HOW TEACHERS
CAN SAVE TEACHERS

Thoughts and Reflections from a Fellow Teacher

GREGORY A. EIBEL

TEACHERS ——✳—— CAN

Limelight Publishing
Lulu Press

Published by Lulu Publishing & Limelight Publishing, 2022

ISBN 978-1-4716-2970-9

Cover design by Lynette Greenfield @ Limelight Publishing.

teacherscansaveteachers.com
limelightpublishing.com
lulu.com

In memory of Matt Malavite.
We talked about writing a book together.
I gave it my best shot.

This book is dedicated to teachers.

We make a difference!

CONTENTS

Part IV: Effecting Change

About The Author

Greg Eibel has been a classroom teacher for 23 years. He has taught social studies, math, science, language arts, and financial literacy in fourth, sixth, seventh, and eighth grades. Currently, he is teaching at-risk students in grades 9-12. Greg has a master's degree, is licensed to teach gifted education, and has a K–12 principal's license. He has served on countless committees, been a department and team leader, and helped in numerous extracurricular activities after school hours. During the past 20 years of his career as an educator, he has coached students from Grades 7 to 12 in golf, football, and track and field. Greg is also president of The Stress Free School Foundation, an organization committed to reducing educator and student stress through consciousness-based educational tools.

teacherscansaveteachers.com

www.stressfreeschoolfoundation.org

PREFACE

This book is a collection of essays covering a variety of topics in education. Some sections may speak to you and your experiences more than others. My hope is that each reader finds an essay that serves them in a positive way. I encourage you to read ahead with an open mind.

Everything that is wrong with education could fill volumes. Everyone has an opinion about school, including me. But for the sake of your time—and sanity—I am keeping this book short and sweet. My hope is that it sparks conversation about change. My dream is for this book to be shared among peers, to bring the topic of change in from the cold. What are the changes we can make as individual teachers in our own classrooms? Can the changes made in our classrooms change the culture of the building or district? Is it possible for us to collectively push for change and reform in the educational system? It's aspirational, but the need for change has never been greater.

Is what you are about to read super insightful? Probably not. Most of what you will read in this book is just common sense. Is it perhaps a little thought-provoking? Maybe even a little helpful? I sure hope so. I believe that sometimes we forget to use the stuff we already know works because some journal or research just came out with a new article on the "real" silver bullet for fixing education. We jump on that bandwagon until the next "real" solution comes along.

I know how valuable time is to teachers, administrators, and support staff. Quite frankly, for many of us, it may be more important than money. Time is a luxury we can't get back. We don't have time to waste. There is too much at stake. There are too many lives that hang in the balance. We must start to make real change before more of our students graduate high school without the ability to handle adversity. They deserve our very best.

INTRODUCTION

Kids love you one day and hate you the next. They hug you on the way in the classroom and throw tantrums on the way out. They lie to their parents and blame you when they get bad grades or get in trouble. Kids have been doing this for as long as there have been schools. However, kids are still the absolute best part of the job. Do they aggravate us and make us want to scream? Sure. They're kids. That's what they do. We can't forget why we chose this profession in the first place. We want to help children learn and prepare them for independence.

I believe that the educational system is focusing on the wrong things. We are focusing on test scores and comparing ourselves to other countries rather than preparing students for a world of rapid change, increasing stress, and general uncertainty about the future of employment. America's students should be learning a foreign language in elementary school. They should be learning how to write code in the early grades. We should focus on the humanities more. We should focus on the arts more. We should focus on the trades more. Of course, reading, writing, math, and science are important, but they're only part of the education kids need.

The stories in the chapters are my own. I was involved in each one. My experiences as a veteran educator have shaped my views and philosophy of education. The stories are told as factually and accurately as I remember. Names and initials have been changed to protect the anonymity of the students and staff involved. I present these stories as anecdotes to provide context for better understanding each topic. I am sure that you have your own stories, and I sincerely hope reading this book brings back some of your best memories.

Use my stories, thoughts, and opinions as fodder for honest conversations that can take place in the open with the right stakeholders. Most of these topics have popped up at the dinner table in my home, while having coffee with colleagues before school, or during team meetings when our frustration level has reached its peak. It is time to take these conversations out of the shadows so we can begin to make some positive changes within our classrooms and our schools. We may not be able to change the system, but we certainly can change what we do as individuals.

I once was asked whether my goal was to completely change the educational system. Honestly, the answer is *yes*—sort of. Though I'm not trying to break down the system and rebuild it myself, I think that, together, we can change the system enough to lessen the constraints of the bureaucratic box we are stuck in. I'm trying to make the box I'm stuck in look like fireworks instead of a dumpster fire. So I'm focusing on what I can control. I have control over my classroom environment and learning that takes place within those four walls. My hope is that you read this book from the perspective of your professional life, as a parent if you are or intend to be one, and simply as a living, breathing human being.

PART I:

Taking Care of Yourself

Chapter 1

Feel Valued

Everyone wants to feel valued and important—to know they have worth. But sometimes, our self-worth is easy to forget. I had been down on myself for quite a while and began wondering whether I was making the difference that inspired me to pursue this profession in the first place. Well, sometimes timing is everything; I received an email from a former student and athlete when I needed it most. I know my former student had no idea how unhappy I was with the teaching profession and that I had been updating my résumé in the days before. It was a typical day in May. I had made up my mind that I was going to be looking really hard over the summer for a new career. I have kept this email in my inbox and refer back to it often. I copied and pasted the email chain here:

Mr. Eibel,

How are you? It's been a while. I hope all is well with you, your family, school, track etc. . . . I am doing pretty good myself, I must say. College is good, finals are over, and I'm going into my last year before I'm officially a licensed Psychologist. I just wanted to make sure things in life were good for you and to let you know that you were one of the biggest influences in my life. I sincerely appreciate you because you always gave me that "extra push" whether it was in academics, athletics, or whatever I was doing. I know you cared, and looking back, I want to say thank you for being a positive male role model in my life. You'll always be someone I look up to (not that you're old or anything) lol.

Thanks a lot,

██████ ██████

██████,

What a surprise to hear from you!! I have to admit that your email couldn't have come at a better time for me. I have had a rough spring . . . nothing bad, just kind of feeling like I'm not making a difference. Then I got your email and it almost brought me to tears to hear you say that I was a positive influence in your life. We teachers don't always know whether or not we make a difference, so thank you! Thank you! Thank you for the email!

I'm so happy to hear that you are on course to graduate. That is fabulous news. I will always be here if you need anything. Take care and stop by and visit if you are in the area.

Greg

I sincerely meant it, Mr. E. You know growing up I didn't have the best childhood, and I RARELY had a positive male role model to look up to. I just wanted someone who cared. I'm glad I could bring a little happiness, man, because I meant every word. I often think of you, but work, school, internships, and life keep me so occupied. As I wrote this email to you, tears fell and that's because you really played an important role in my becoming the young man I am today. I can truly say that I came a long way despite all my trials, barriers, and life just being difficult. In a few semesters, I'll be done. And, no, thank YOU for caring because in certain times in my life I felt as if no one did. Life threw me a major curveball, but I didn't let it define nor defeat me. I feel very accomplished, and I feel as if my brother and sisters are going to be so proud of me (that's really who I am doing all this for). I will be sure to let you know when I do come back to town. Maybe we can go sit and eat or something. You have a safe, prosperous, good, enjoyable summer. I'll keep in touch.

███████

Well thank you anyway. I'm very proud of you!!! And more importantly, you should be proud of yourself.

G

I'm sure most of us have received a message like this at some point in our careers. When things were going well, you probably thought, "Aw, that's nice. I needed that." However, when things seem like they are collapsing all around you, a message like that, at that time, is worth more than gold. It's like the voicemail you just aren't ready to delete; not quite yet. Maybe you made a copy or keep the original in a desk drawer, but you refer back to it when you need it. We all make a difference. The question we have to ask ourselves is, what kind of difference do we want to make?

What makes us feel important is different for everyone. Some of us need affirmation. Others may need purpose. Some people need to lead, and others are happy to contribute in their own way. Regardless of the role, everyone needs to feel important in some aspect of their lives. Whether at home, at work, or in school, people (including children) who feel valued are happier and more productive.

How many times have you watched your students' faces light up when they became the teacher and showed a peer how to do something? How about when they earned their first "A" or when you complimented them for a particular behavior in class? Perhaps you made a positive phone call home, and they came in the next morning beaming with pride. The upshot of all these strategies is students who feel valued and, more than likely, go on to have a pretty good day. They may even embrace the positive changes and be willing to continue to do things that make them feel worthwhile. We have to celebrate their accomplishments to keep that feeling of value alive.

Everyone Succeeds

One of the keys to helping kids feel that they can learn is to start the school year with a lesson so easy that everyone can achieve success. Then be sure to take a moment to celebrate that success with your students. Go over the top, if needed, but get the kids to believe they can learn. If you do that, they will buy into what you are selling. Moreover, this simple acknowledgment will help them feel their own value. This approach works in any subject, at any grade level, and at any point in your students' education.

Instructional and assessment strategies can have a direct impact on our students' feelings of value. I teach middle school social studies. For about 10 years, I have started the school year with the students learning the 50 states, regardless of whether I was teaching sixth, seventh, or eighth grade. We always start the year that way. Some years, we're done with the whole country in a week; other years, it takes the whole semester.

Please don't think that this is all we do during that time. We hit the practice hard in the first week, then taper off as new topics and lessons are added. It doesn't matter how long it takes;

my students are going to learn their states so they can never say, "Mr. Eibel didn't teach me anything."

I use this content because it's one that provides for universal rates of success, regardless of their prior knowledge, whether they have a learning disability, or whether they are gifted. If they practice enough times using enough different methods, students will learn the states. My job is pretty simple: I just have to find as many different ways as I can for students to practice identifying each state. I like to break down the states into regions and just teach eight to 10 states at a time. My biggest fear is pushing students to frustration by forcing them to learn all 50 at a time. Maybe identifying the location of 20 states is the right number for some kids. Maybe high-achieving students compete against one another or the clock to determine who can correctly identify the states the fastest.

In addition, I allow them as many attempts as they need until they get an "A." Several students find their own ways to practice, and they share those methods with their peers, making my job even easier. My "real" job is to make the kids feel valuable and important. I do this by celebrating their success. If I see that they are getting frustrated with quizzes, I give them the option to identify the states in their own way and give them credit for what they know.

This tactic is certainly not a novel idea, and I readily admit that I don't have all the answers. You know the students in your classroom. The experts don't, the politicians and bureaucrats don't, and tragically, some of their parents don't either. I know that's horrible to say, but it is the unfortunate truth for too many kids. This idea is just something that works for me. You will find what works for yourself and use it to start off your school year on the right foot. Don't expect the first thing you try to be the lucky charm. It took me about 10 years before I tried teaching the states during the first weeks of school. If you are a social studies teacher and want to use this trick in your classroom, by all means do so. We don't need to reinvent the wheel. My hope is that you keep trying new ideas throughout the year until something works.

Sometimes helping kids to feel valued and improve their self-worth is extremely challenging. Don't forget that life is a marathon, not a sprint. The more times children have the experiences of feeling valued, the more likely their belief in themselves will take hold and grow. Celebrate the little wins—not just for the students, but for yourself as well. You are making a difference. You are doing more good than you realize.

A colleague had a warm-up assignment to start class in which she asked students to explain why one of their teachers would be on Santa's "nice" list this year.

This was one of the responses she received:

Mr. Ebil

- He spent lots of time helping us and letting us speak to him.
- He made sure that we learned while he was also very caring for us.
- He loved teaching us and being kind to others.

There isn't a Mr. Ebil that works in my building so I'm going to assume this note is about me even though the spelling of the name is a little off. We should all strive to make this type of difference in our classrooms. The context is important here; the student wrote this about me after I was away from him for 2 months on medical leave. This is what he remembered about me. I'm not sharing this to toot my own horn. I just want you to see that we are all making a difference even when we don't realize it. By the time he was asked to write for this prompt, he literally had the substitute teacher for more days than he had me as a teacher. You can change a life in a split second. Believe me, you can, in a positive or negative way.

Everyone Makes Mistakes

Keep in mind that students may not remember what you taught them, but they will remember how you treated them. That includes both the good and the bad, unfortunately. Making students feel valued is of utmost importance. However, we must keep in mind that our words and actions can have the opposite effect. While writing this book, I wrestled with how much of my life I wanted to share. Writing about the successful strategies I have implemented is easy, but it is only half the story. I have made countless mistakes throughout my career. Yet, my mistakes frequently taught me more than my successes. Therefore, I decided to share some of my failures as well so that you may avoid making the same mistakes I've made.

One of those mistakes happened during my time as the head varsity track coach. I ran track in high school and college and still love the sport. In my view, coaching is just teaching, and teaching is just coaching. Coaching can bring out the absolute best in you, but it can also bring out the absolute worst. Even if you haven't ever coached, I think you will understand the point of the story.

Sometimes in sports you have an unbelievably talented roster. Most of the time, your roster is just average. From time to time, no matter what you do, the other team's Jimmys are better than your Joes. In other words, you are just outmatched. As a coach, I believe our number one job is to help kids learn about life through sports. Though winning is a very, very close second.

Regardless of what type of roster a coach has, there are three ways the season can go. Your athletes can come together as a team and overachieve. This is by far the most fun you will have coaching and what we all strive to accomplish.

The second scenario for coaches is the most common: Your team achieves at the level it should.

The third is what I call the Coach's Graveyard. This is the type of season that drives coaches out of the profession, never to return to coaching.

My greatest regret in coaching happened when I had a talented roster, and the team was coming together. We had the potential to have a very special season. But I made a big mistake with a former athlete that has bothered me ever since.

We were facing the one team that could prevent us from winning the Conference Championship. Track coaches have all kinds of contingency plans to draw from if we need to move around athletes during events. I had a very good distance runner that season, and I was counting on him to score points in all three distance races. However, there was no contingency plan for when he told me he couldn't run that day. I thought he was joking, but he was dead serious.

I was caught by surprise and couldn't understand why he wasn't able to run in the biggest meet of the year. The team was counting on every member to contribute because it was the only way we could win. I asked whether he could just gut out the first race and see what happens. He was adamant that he would not be running that day.

I pleaded with him. I asked what was wrong and whether there was anything I could do to help him. Was he sick? Was he hurt? He just said he couldn't run. That's when I lost my cool because I just couldn't figure out what would keep him from running. It was so frustrating because he wasn't giving me any insight. I looked him right in the eye and said, "That's cowardly. Your team needs you, and you aren't even gonna try? That's b#$*@t." And I walked away.

In that split second, I broke a relationship, lost the confidence of my team, and turned a promising season into a dumpster fire. I mentioned that no matter what type of roster you have, the season can go three ways. We had the potential to be the talented team that came together and overachieved. Unfortunately, I turned my talented team into a dysfunctional mess with one sharp comment made in frustration. I ruined a relationship with a really nice kid and turned the season into a disappointment for the other kids on the team. It was my fault, and mine alone. Not my finest moment in coaching, or life for that matter.

We have to find ways to keep our cool in the midst of what may seem like chaos, because as soon as we lose control and let something slip in frustration, we may unintentionally ruin a relationship. What kids observe and remember is amazing. Things that you and I dismiss as nonevents might be the things they remember about you for the rest of their life. I bet you have a story about a teacher that did something to make you upset.

I bet you still remember it like it happened the other day. Unfortunately, you might not remember too many good things that the teacher did, or tried to do for you, because of that one moment.

As a teacher and coach, I have had bad days where something a kid did upset me. While trying to resolve certain situations, I have said or done things in frustration that I never meant to do or say, but it happened because of stress, frustration, or anger. No amount of apologizing will help them forget what I said or did. We are going to make mistakes. The key is to limit the damage done by those mistakes. That is why it is more important than ever to reduce our stress (the topic of Chapter 2) so we can remain calm and clear-headed in the midst of chaos. We can make a positive impact just as quickly as a negative one.

Your Turn

Help your students feel valued.

This authentic activity is beneficial both for you and your students. Have each student write the name of every person in the class, including yours. Beside each name, have students write the nicest thing they can think about each of their classmates and about you. Do the same for each of your students. Collect all the papers and make individual lists for each student of all the nice things their peers said about them; compile your own list as well. You could add a technology component to this if you wish to teach students about positive ways to communicate online or through social media.

My reflections:

_____

_____

_____

_____

_____

_____

_____

_____

_____

_____

_____

_____

_____

Steps to maximize my potential:

_____

_____

_____

_____

_____

_____

_____

_____

_____

_____

_____

_____

Chapter 2

Reduce Stress

Stress is the single biggest factor holding us back from our true potential. Stress is a sneaky thing that impacts every aspect of our life, from our health, to our marriage, to how we raise and teach our own children, to our relationships with others. Furthermore, stress affects us professionally.

People are more productive when their minds are clear and they can focus on the tasks ahead. It's that simple.

Most of us do not realize how stressed we are because it builds on itself, adding layer upon layer. The danger of stress is that if we don't find ways to manage it, we may begin to forget what it feels like to live without it. Perhaps you know you are stressed, but you just don't realize how stressed you actually are. To my mind, my stress was just the reality of my life, so I did what most of us do and tried to find ways to manage the stress myself.

Self-Medicating

We all have stress, and we all self-medicate. For me, I turned to eating and drinking. Social drinking became my form of self-medication. I rarely have a drink at home and never fell into the routine of having one or two after work; but I was definitely excited when there was a social event. In fact, I planned many of them so I could have a reason to blow off steam.

Maybe this pattern resonates with you. Perhaps social drinking is your crutch as well. If you're anything like me, the party provides a distraction for a short time, but it doesn't address the root problems causing the stress. After the fun is over, do you wake up the next morning feeling free of stress? Perhaps you feel even worse depending on how much fun the party was. The question I want you to reflect on is: Are you a good spouse, parent, and/or teacher the next day? It's great if you are, but I would argue that it is just a temporary fix to a much deeper issue. What is helping you manage the stress, not just of your job, but of your life?

Managing Stress

I assume you head home at the end of the day to your family, perhaps to very young children. Maybe you are in grad school working to advance your career while working full-time. Perhaps you coach a sport. Maybe you are the band or choir director. We all give our time to others in one way or another. Regardless, stress finds us all at various points in our lives, and we have to find outlets to release it. You have your hands full and are spinning many plates; stress relief is essential.

Of course, everyone is different, and we all manage stress in our own way. Maybe, like me, you turn to drinking or eating. The health-conscious reader may focus on exercise or a hobby (both great ways to reduce stress). Maybe you need drugs, prescription or otherwise. I am in no position to judge your stress management techniques, whatever they may be. All I am here to do is offer an alternative for you to consider.

I have found that meditation has checked all the boxes I am looking for to manage my stress. I basically have stopped drinking; I only have one or two drinks in social settings rather than my usual four to six or sometimes more. Reducing my stress led me to eat and drink less; I lost more than 20 pounds and feel so much better. Meditation has been proven by science to reduce stress.

Avoiding Burnout

The staff and administrators in my building are stressed out. Numerous personal and professional pressures are causing stress in our lives. Unfortunately, our stress is sometimes projected onto the students, and that directly impacts learning. For students, their stress manifests in their refusal to do anything. When they reach their frustration point, they prefer to look like they don't care rather than to try and fail. Something has to be done to help relieve some of that stress and anxiety so we can get back to the basic tenet of this job: building lifelong learners who are hardworking, productive, responsible citizens—not just good test takers. There isn't an easy answer. But if we continue on our current trajectory, I fear we may not recover.

How many of us are figuratively counting the days until retirement? Some of you may be literally counting the days. Teaching is a difficult job that can lead to burnout. A colleague recently asked me whether I thought stress equals burnout. I didn't have an answer at the time, but I have thought about it since. To the best of my knowledge, there is good stress, bad stress, and all variations in between. I have come to the conclusion that not managing stress is what leads to burnout. In the right circumstances, stress can lead to phenomenal human achievements. However, if not managed properly, it absolutely can lead to burnout and serious health problems.

Reducing your stress can help you better manage your daily life. We all want to get to retirement, but at what expense? Our health? Our energy levels? Our passion? Our energy, passion, and health may decline with age, but we can use knowledge and experience to make up for what declines if we reduce our stress levels. The best teachers have wisdom, passion, and energy, but these are hard to maintain year after year. Each year that passes brings us closer to retirement. Are you enjoying the years that are flying by so fast? Are you really willing to sacrifice youth, energy, and vitality for retirement? Or would you rather enjoy life now, knowing that tomorrow is never guaranteed? If talented teachers get so stressed or burned out that they decide to leave the profession, what are we left with? What will be the state of education in our country, and how will it affect society?

About Meditation

As best as historians can pinpoint, meditation has been around for more than 5,000 years. People have been meditating in similar ways for millenia. How can a "fad" last for thousands of years? Obviously, it can't. So there must be something to this technique. Science is just starting to catch up by researching how and why these processes work. If you're skeptical, as well you should be, I would like to point out that something that has been around for 5,000 years must work, and more importantly, have value. Maybe the ancients didn't understand why or how, but they knew that it was worthwhile. Science is just proving what they already knew.

Meditation is a broad and somewhat difficult concept to define. According to the Cleveland Clinic, the practice of meditation "involves focusing or clearing your mind using a combination of mental and physical techniques."[1] Some techniques use repeated mantras or sounds to help clear the mind. Others use mindfulness, or focusing the mind on an object, thought, or activity. Regardless of the technique you use,

---

[1] The Cleveland Clinic provides a nice overview of meditation on their website if you would like more information.

meditation has been proven to reduce stress, anxiety and depression.

Within the past few decades, modern technologies, such as EEG and MRI, have allowed doctors and scientists to conduct research into the effects of meditation on the brain and physiology. Scientists are learning more each day about the positive effects meditation has on the brain and nervous system. The results from earlier research have led to new and ongoing studies to help doctors understand the effects of meditation on cardiovascular health, as well as treating autism, ADHD, and PTSD.

There are different forms of meditation that use different techniques to achieve a more relaxed state of mind. Many people make the choice to meditate so they can reduce stress and anxiety. Others find meditation improves their overall health or leads them to higher states of consciousness. For me personally, I have found an overall sense of peace and more clarity of thought. I will be discussing the form of meditation I chose later in the book.

Your Turn

Help yourself reduce stress.

Take the first 30 minutes when you get home for yourself. If that doesn't work for you, find those 30 minutes before school. You spend all day and evening giving yourself out to everyone else. All I am asking is that you take back a minimum of 30 minutes a day for yourself. These are just a few of the things I have done to manage my stress:

- Practice yoga.
- Take a walk.
- Play with a pet.
- Listen to music.
- Work on a puzzle.
- Read.

I like art, so my wife bought me a paint-by-number kit. It was very satisfying, and it took my mind off whatever was bothering me. It was especially helpful to paint and listen to music at the same time.

Limit your screen time before bed.

My reflections:

_____
_____
_____
_____
_____
_____
_____
_____
_____
_____
_____
_____
_____

Steps to maximize my potential:

_____
_____
_____
_____
_____
_____
_____
_____
_____
_____
_____
_____

Chapter 3

Embrace Change

For many of us, *change* is one of the scariest words in the dictionary. In terms of education, I want to try to put change into perspective. Think about a time in your life when you felt like everything around you was collapsing and your world was falling apart. I bet you were feeling that way because something (other than the death of a loved one) was changing in your life and the experience was horrible. When the trauma subsided, looking back on that time with a clear mind, can you say that the change, as horrible as it may have been, actually led you to a better place? Maybe it hasn't happened quite yet, but you probably aren't feeling as bad about it now as you once did.

CHANGE BEYOND OUR CONTROL

When one change happened to me, I certainly didn't see it as a good thing. I was furious and literally ready to quit teaching altogether. The change just didn't make any sense to me.

Here's what happened. For a brief few years, I had my absolute dream job in teaching. I was teaching seventh- and eighth-grade social studies with a great team of teachers and interventionists. Our social studies department was very strong, and things felt like they were really heading in the right direction.

I am a history nerd who loves all the stories of history regardless of time period, continent, culture, and the like. I believe that to truly understand history, you must learn the stories of all cultures and time periods because they are connected to the history of mankind. Certain periods of time, however, are more interesting to me than others. Personally, I am fascinated by early American history, particularly colonization through the Civil War. My standards in eighth grade focused on that exact time period, so I felt very comfortable teaching the content. In seventh grade I was teaching my other passions: Ancient Greece and Rome, the Middle Ages, and the Renaissance/Reformation. I would have been content teaching these classes for the rest of my career and probably would have been very happy.

You likely are aware that each year in the winter and spring, administrators are planning for the next school year. I don't know exactly what goes into that, but I assume they look at programs, class sizes, retirements and resignations, teaming of teachers and interventionists, teacher licensure, and certainly more. When one change gets made, it can unfortunately start a chain of unintended consequences. It could also lead to something better if we just give it time to play out. Though we don't know what will happen in the end, we can keep an open mind when looking at change.

As a result of some changes being made at the high school, a teacher was transferred to the middle school. Her license allowed her to teach only Grades 7 through 12 social studies so I was bumped to sixth grade social studies to make room for her. This was nobody's fault. It was just something that had to happen. At the time, I didn't understand that. I blamed everyone and was ready to update my résumé.

LOOKING BACK

I might have saved myself a lot of grief had I embraced the change at the onset. It turns out that the teacher who moved to the middle school is a wonderful woman and is working really hard to help the students learn the content. I'm happy that she is at our school now.

For me, moving to sixth grade turned out to be great. I have formed some close friendships with different colleagues, I have learned more of the human story by studying new content, and I have a better appreciation for the maturity and development of middle school students.

If we can hold our emotions in check and think rationally and logically about change, we might be able to see the benefits, not just the negatives. Realizing this truth took me a long time, and I made a mess of mandated changes most of the time. Change is scary, but it isn't always bad. Things always seem to work out in the end. We usually figure it out. We learn from it. We become more resilient because of it.

Why We Resist Change

I believe we resist change for two reasons: fear and selfishness. I want to talk about fear first. Fear of the unknown is a powerful emotion. It prevents us from taking risks, and it prevents us from fulfilling our true potential. Overcoming this fear is easier said than done. As discussed earlier, we know that change can turn out for the best. With some help, discussed next, we can work on overcoming our fear of change because we know that it will be okay, maybe even better, in the end.

The second reason is selfishness. GUILTY! I am guilty of this as well. If you're anything like me, you might worry about how this is going to affect you. I know that I do. But this isn't about me, and I hate to break it to you, it isn't about you either. It isn't about any one child or any one parent. This is about the collective good of our children.

Leaving Our Comfort Zone

For me personally, change happened by hitting me with a sledgehammer because I really didn't see it coming. But I believe that a simple technique can help us think clearly, even in the midst of change or trauma.

Meditation helped me to see this situation as just another change in life. Now, when I think back to terrible experiences I have had, change doesn't scare me anymore because I know that everything will work out for the better. I still experience moments of doubt, sadness, anger, and anxiety, but these feelings don't linger. They don't overwhelm me. I see them as just inconveniences designed to slow me up from fulfilling my potential. Though we may be afraid to get out of our comfort zone, we can't be afraid of change. Sometimes that comfort zone leads to complacency and even burnout.

Embracing Change

Changes in education have taken place since the beginning of time. We've come a long way from one-room schoolhouses with outhouses, chalkboards, Ditto machines, and textbooks to the Internet, email, social media, and online learning. Change is inevitable. So, we can either let it consume us, or we can embrace it and help influence what changes are made. It's up to us to fight for the right changes and to create the educational system that is best for our students.

As teachers, we advocate for the collective good of all kids. We are passionate about providing the next generation with the best options and preparation for their lives. We are living the lives we chose, and that is because we had a lot of help along the way. We can pay it forward by giving our students the schools they deserve. Each of us brings something to the table. Collectively, we can use our brain power, talent, goodwill, and creativity to offer our students our very best.

Open yourself to embrace change. Or would you prefer to go back to 19" TVs with antennae and typewriters? I would gladly give up the Encyclopedia Britannica I had when I was growing up for the power of the Internet.

Change is coming whether we want it or not. It may be a minor change or could be a full overhaul. The only thing I am asking of you is to use logic and common sense to make sure that the change is what you believe is right. Don't fear it. Use it to your benefit, and remember that things always work out in the end.

Your Turn

Help yourself by helping others.

For me, personally, change has always been difficult. The one thing that has always helped me cope with change is helping others. It may seem weird, but when I am deliberately thinking about or trying to help someone else, I end up coping with the change that is happening in my life. We have all heard the adage "It's better to give than receive." Helping others is a form of giving, and the benefits of doing so are immeasurable. The next time change is causing you stress, try to find a way to help someone in need. You don't need to make some grand gesture; even the smallest helpful hand will suffice.

My reflections:

_____
_____
_____
_____
_____
_____
_____
_____
_____
_____
_____
_____

Steps to maximize my potential:

_____
_____
_____
_____
_____
_____
_____
_____
_____
_____
_____
_____

PART II:

OVERCOMING RESTRAINTS

CHAPTER 4

USE YOUR OWN EXPERTISE

One of the things that has always driven me nuts about educational experts, leaders in the field, politicians, and bureaucrats is that they always claim to have the right answers. I always have thought to myself: If you have all the answers, or this works so well, why aren't you putting it into practice? I do believe they truly mean well, but here is what I have concluded about experts:

- There is no such thing.
- Anyone who claims to be an expert is probably just trying to sell you something.
- We are all just trying to do the best we can with the tools, knowledge, and experience we have.

Gaining Expertise

In his book *Outliers: The Story of Success,* Malcolm Gladwell asserts that it takes 10,000 hours of practice to become an expert at anything. Ten thousand hours! That got me thinking about my own career. How many hours have I spent teaching? I wonder whether I'm an expert. Haha!

No way; not even close. Having a tendency to overthink things, I got out my calculator and started doing the math. I wanted to be very conservative just to see the absolute minimum number of hours I could have spent actually teaching. Then I took it a step further, because I really overthink things, and tried to figure out how many hours I have coached.

Here are the numbers I used; remember this is being as conservative as I can be. I'm certain that I have taught and coached significantly more than this. For you math teachers out there, here is my formula:

- Number of hours teaching = 23 years × 160 days × 5 hours
- I have an absolute minimum of 18,400 hours teaching in my career. Am I an expert? Hardly.

- Number of hours coaching = 20 years × 140 days × 2 hours
- I have an absolute minimum of 5,600 hours of coaching in my career. In all honesty, it is probably closer to 10,000 hours because I didn't factor in the length of competitions. I just used 2 hours per day as an average. Nevertheless, it still confirms that I'm definitely not an expert at coaching.

I'm not telling you this to prove that I am an expert and should be taken seriously; quite the opposite actually. I DO NOT consider myself an expert in anything. I'm just a guy who is trying to get better each and every day. I wonder whether all the so-called experts have put their theory into practice for 10,000 hours.

CONSIDERING THE X FACTOR

Telling people what to do and how to do it is really easy. Actually doing it is a heck of a lot harder especially when all these theories sound great, but don't take into account the X factor. Nobody really knows what is going to happen in a classroom on any given day (the X factor). Many of these theories don't take that into account. They are designed for a utopia. Unfortunately, we do not live in a utopian world, so teachers have to be ready to adjust at a moment's notice. I haven't heard a lot of experts give thoughts and suggestions for how to use their strategies when kids don't take their medication one day, or their parents are getting a divorce and the home life is a mess, or any of the numerous other things that can happen during the school day.

Using Qualitative Data

Data. It's the necessary evil. When used properly, data is essential to success. Some data is quantitative and some is qualitative. I believe education should live in the world of qualitative data. Unfortunately, our educational system lives in the quantitative world most of the time. It's all about the numbers.

Of course data is valuable, but we need to be collecting the right type of data. Data can also be skewed. We all have probably seen examples of one side claiming data that supports their point of view, while the other side claims data to oppose that view. Who are we supposed to believe? We probably end up believing the data that supports our beliefs, values, or gut instinct. Is that data valid? Who knows?

Data is tricky and is often used to sell an idea, theory, or perspective. Unfortunately, we can't just trust the data. We have to use experiences, knowledge, wisdom, common sense, and other ways to measure success. These are children, not numbers. That's why I'm proposing that we take a look at how we can use more qualitative data in schools, rather than primarily quantitative data. I assure you that I really do understand the importance of data, but I also see the need to improve how we measure student learning.

A Swinging Pendulum

Most new ideas that experts come up with aren't new at all. These strategies and techniques have been around forever. Experts just take something that already existed, rename it, polish it up a little bit, and claim they have the answer to our problem. Think about this: Teachers in one-room schoolhouses were using differentiated instruction before it was called that. They were teaching English as a second language to many immigrant children. They were creating individualized education plans for kids (they called that curriculum). They had behavior management plans. They were using RtI (Response to Intervention). They just called it "figuring out a different way to help the students learn." The biggest difference is they didn't have to do all the paperwork that is required now.

Speaking of paperwork, hasn't it gotten a little out of hand? I digress, though. Most of what works has been around for generations; it just had a different name. I know it is a cliché (ugh), but we all know that the definition of insanity is doing the same thing over and over and expecting a different result. Isn't that exactly what we have been doing? Are we insane?

Those of you who have been in education for a significant amount of time know that the pendulum just keeps swinging back and forth. For those of you new to the profession, here's a quick lesson: The philosophy or idea that is fresh, and new, and exciting right now won't be in a few years. Politicians and bureaucrats will create policies that swing the pendulum in the opposite direction. When it swings back, you will see the same ideas, but with different names or acronyms.

Alphabet Soup

One question I often reflect on is this. Why do you have to have letters at the end of your name (MEd, PhD, EdD) to be taken seriously in our society? My mechanic doesn't have any letters after his name, except maybe Jr. All I know is that guy is an expert when it comes to something I don't know how to do. Socrates, Plato, and Aristotle were forward thinkers, who sometimes were viewed as lunatics. They didn't have diplomas, or licenses, or advanced degrees. They just had their experience and brains.

Within all of us is a sixth sense that lets us know when something doesn't feel quite right. Some people may refer to it as consciousness, intuition, or perhaps a conscience. Regardless of what we call it, there is in fact something inside us that is designed to protect us from danger.

In addition to protecting us from danger, our sixth sense, which I'm going to call *pure consciousness,* is also the center of our creativity, knowledge, and joy. Imagine being able to tap into your center of creativity and knowledge to solve problems in your classroom, make daily decisions, plan engaging lessons, or improve your relationships with students and colleagues. It is possible. Meditation is a technique that can help every human tap into pure consciousness to be able to live a more peaceful, productive, and happy life.

Your Turn

Help yourself by learning from others.

Meet with a teacher in your building that you respect and believe does an outstanding job teaching students. Have a conversation with that person about his or her philosophies, how relationships with students are formed, and strategies for areas where you want to improve. You have experts right in your building. You just have to seek them out.

My reflections:

_____
_____
_____
_____
_____
_____
_____
_____
_____
_____
_____

Steps to maximize my potential:

_____
_____
_____
_____
_____
_____
_____
_____
_____
_____
_____

Chapter 5

Make Your Voice Heard

I want to preface this chapter by saying that politicians and bureaucrats are well-meaning people. I believe most of them have the best interest of others at heart. However, they are not the ones who have to accomplish what is being required. If you trust politicians, then you probably agree that education needs to be fixed, and perhaps they have the right answers. But if you're like me, you might be led to believe that the people making decisions about education, the ones behind the scenes, the policy makers, are ruining education. I don't believe they are doing it intentionally, but they ARE ruining it with policies that are forcing teachers and schools to assume the role of a parent, but don't support them in their efforts to do so.

Responsibility Without Authority

We are not our students' parents, but oftentimes it feels like we are responsible for raising these children and developing their social, emotional, mental, physical, and academic well-being. We are supposed to help them with every aspect of their lives, like a parent should, but without the authority to discipline or consequence them. The teachers don't have the rights. The kids have all the rights. Therefore, teachers are unable to assume a parental role because half the tools in their toolbag have been taken from them by some ridiculous policies. The more policy makers promise to fix education, the more they screw it up. We absolutely must get politics out of the educational system!

Preserving Ideals

The summer before fifth grade, my parents took my sister and me to Washington, DC, for the first time. That trip started my fascination with history. We did all the usual tourist things in and around Washington, but the thing that sticks out the most for me is getting to meet our U.S. Representative, Ralph Regula.

Congressman Regula took us on a tour of his office building, the Capitol, and the House of Representatives. He couldn't have been more kind and generous with his time. That experience made me want to be a politician because I saw his job as a way to make things better for everyone, and that appealed to me. I was 10, so forgive my naïveté, but I saw politicians as people who had the best interest of the country at heart.

Times were different back then. It was the 1980s, and America was still fighting Communism and the Cold War. The biggest fear was the threat of nuclear war, not terrorism per se. There were plane hijackings and bombings in other parts of the world, but those events were far away and the media was very different, so they didn't affect us much. Maybe it was the fact that I was a kid, but even though the world was dangerous, America didn't seem dangerous. We had pride in our country. We believed that we would always win because we were the bright, shining light spreading freedom and democracy around the world. At least that is what we were taught and told. The world is very complicated. As a result, we don't always get it right, but I believe we still hold those ideals.

Times have changed, but those ideals have not. I definitely DO NOT want to be a politician now, but for a long time I saw it as a way to help people. Politics has ruined a system that, for what it's worth, has led the world and been the envy of the world for generations. Is our educational system perfect? No, of course not. But, I wonder why countries are sending their kids to our schools and universities and modeling their system after ours? I argue that for all that's wrong with it, our system is still the best. We can't afford to let it continue to head in the direction it is going.

Examining the Policies

Public education needs to make a drastic and fundamental shift in our thinking about how we do business, and it starts with eliminating the policy makers and bureaucrats at every level. Unfortunately, many of them are in it for themselves and see their policy as a stepping stone to a better position. Everyone wants to introduce a new idea so they can become known and use it to climb the professional ladder. After those politicians or bureaucrats climb the ladder, we are stuck with a pile of thoughts, theories, and policies that were shoved through without careful examination and are still on the books years, perhaps decades later.

How do we fix the system? I will be the first to say that I don't have all the answers, but something I think could help is to examine the policies and mandates. If they don't work, they should go. Next, I propose forming a commission at the highest level in each state. We should invite designers, business leaders, financial leaders, and manufacturing leaders to participate. Furthermore, we should include representatives from the blue and white collar sectors, the gig economy (short-term, freelance-based workers such as Uber or Airbnb), the service industry, the trades, and the arts. We need to find the CEOs and business owners with the knowledge and foresight to help figure out what our educational system can do to prepare kids for the type of work American companies may need in the future. I do not believe politicians and bureaucrats should have a say in the implementation process. Each commission on education should give its recommendations to its state board of education and let the state or individual districts figure out how to implement them.

I believe this approach would make a huge difference in the quality of education. We need to take some of the power from the policy makers, academics, and bureaucrats who work in theory rather than practicality. We can do better as an educational system, and it starts by contacting your elected representatives and letting them know how you feel.

Your Turn

Help your school by contacting your local, state, and federal elected representatives.

They all have email contact forms. You don't have to say much. Just say what's on your mind. It doesn't even have to be about education. The only way we can implement change in a democracy is by making our voices heard. You personally don't have to be loud. If we have enough voices, the volume will increase. Your students have every right, and should be encouraged to contact their representatives as well. This could be a great civics lesson for them.

My reflections:

_____
_____
_____
_____
_____
_____
_____
_____
_____
_____
_____

Steps to maximize my potential:

_____
_____
_____
_____
_____
_____
_____
_____
_____
_____
_____

CHAPTER 6

AVOID THE TESTING QUICKSAND

Continuing my rant from the previous chapter, I would like to focus my wrath on testing next. It is one of the biggest wastes of taxpayer money in history. What has it shown? I'll tell you: It has shown that our kids can either read and comprehend tests or they can't.

Looking Back

Please forgive my memory of this next story because I'm not sure how accurate my facts are, but this is how I remember it. I was a freshman in high school during the 1990–1991 school year. We had taken standardized tests at various times leading up to that point in my school career, but they never meant anything to us. We were told my freshman year that we had to pass a Proficiency Test in order to graduate. This is where my memory is a little fuzzy, but I believe we were the first graduating class where the Proficiency Test was a mandate for graduation. My friends and I were all nervous about this test. We did well in school and were all on the college preparatory path. That would all come to a crashing end if we didn't pass this test. There was a lot of pressure on us.

I can't remember a single question, but I do remember thinking that if you can't pass this test, you probably shouldn't graduate. The mandate stated that once a student passed the Proficiency Test, they were done with it until senior year. Students who did not pass as a freshman would have opportunities to retest throughout the remainder of high school. As a senior, we were required to take a Proficiency Test again to determine whether we were eligible for an Honors Diploma.

That's really all I remember about the Proficiency Test. Maybe it was too easy; I don't know. It Just seemed like a fair test that you should be able to pass if you want to graduate from high school. That testing model has certainly shifted in the past 30 years. I'm all for raising the bar and raising our standards and expectations, but not at the expense of the social, emotional, and mental health of children.

Measuring Growth

Today's testing environment is significantly different from the Proficiency Test I took. I don't remember the Proficiency Test measuring whether I grew a year in school. What is a year's growth anyway? What does that even mean? So are we all supposed to grow and mature and learn at the exact same pace? It's ridiculous! It's just something a bureaucrat or academic came up with based on a set of standards, benchmarks, or indicators they created. It certainly wasn't a doctor or a parent, who I think understands that all kids grow and mature at different paces.

Why then do we expect all children to come into school and fit into the same mold of a year's growth? That isn't even remotely logical. It doesn't even take into account what their home life is like, their starting level at the beginning of the year, or the culture of the school. We can't boil down learning to a year's growth. Learning occurs in many different ways over the course of a lifetime. That's why our singular focus should be to develop children into lifetime learners. It should be that simple.

In my opinion, state tests are not age or grade-level appropriate anymore. Politicians and bureaucrats want to be able to say, "Look at how challenging our tests are. We are raising expectations. We are raising the bar." I am all for raising the bar, but here is what has actually happened. On paper these tests look like they are challenging our students. Yet, actually, they are far above the actual level of many students. In reality, they are just causing stress and general dislike of any type of assessment.

Appropriately Leveling the Tests

I'm not sure whether anybody truly understands how these standardized tests are scored. To the best of my knowledge, the range of scores is based on how all the students scored on the test that particular year. When the scores are based on a mean or median of all scores, that doesn't really show proficiency or growth. The results just show the mean or median score and how all the students rank compared to that score. To me, a passing or proficient score shouldn't be determined by how other students are doing, but how each individual student performs.

This is what I mean when I say that these tests are not leveled appropriately. If we have to continue to use testing as a way to hold schools and teachers accountable, let's create a fair and appropriate test where student learning is measured in smaller chunks, rather than one big yearly test, and where proficiency is actually measured. Make the passing score 70%, but make it actually achievable.

I feel that state tests don't measure a student's learning at all. A student might have a successful year and grow at more than a year's growth, but have a rough test day. We can't base a student's learning on a couple of tests each year. They're kids.

They have rough days just like we do. I certainly do not want to be judged as a teacher based on my principal coming into my class on the worst day of the year. How is that fair? If we have to use tests, we need to look into a more diagnostic system that is progressive and truly shows what kids are learning and are able to do. The tests may not show proficiency according to state testing requirements, but will be a better tool for measuring what students have learned and what teachers have taught them.

Testing has created an epidemic of stress in schools. Not just for the kids, but for teachers, administrators, support staff, school boards, and even parents. The only people not stressed by testing are the politicians, bureaucrats, and educational companies who profit from this system.

Reconsidering Current Testing

Politicians have been bought and paid for by contributions from giant educational conglomerates who see testing as a way to make money by creating and selling tests to states. They make even more money by creating the course material needed to pass the tests, and in turn selling it to the states. It might be time to reconsider this testing path we are on. Maybe we've been sold a bill of goods.

Your Turn

Help yourself by accepting what you can control.

I would like to give you two strategies this time. First, spend some time managing your stress in a healthy way this week. Second, make a list of all the things wrong with the testing system. You don't have to write an article or a paper about it. Making a list may be a cathartic exercise for you. You will begin to realize just how many things are out of your control. By understanding what you can and cannot control, you may begin to make peace with your role in education. You can't fix every problem, but you can make a positive impact in the lives of your students on a daily basis.

My reflections:

_____

_____

_____

_____

_____

_____

_____

_____

_____

_____

_____

Steps to maximize my potential:

_____

_____

_____

_____

_____

_____

_____

_____

_____

_____

_____

PART III:

Reaching All Your Students

Chapter 7

Challenge Your Gifted Students

In my experience, gifted students are the most underserved students in our schools. Yes, they usually get good grades, and yes, they usually pass the state tests, but they rarely achieve more than a year's growth in each grade. They are not being given the opportunity to reach their potential. Instead, they are being pulled toward the middle and mediocrity. The majority of attention is being spent trying to make sure that all the other kids can pass the test. The gifted population is among the students we know will pass. We just want to make sure they learn the content so they don't mess up on the state tests. What a missed opportunity!

Learning Outside the Classroom

A few years ago, Walmart® offered school grants for the cost of transportation to and from the Ohio General Assembly (our statehouse). I saw this as an amazing opportunity to take learning out of the classroom for my high-achieving social studies students. I was fortunate to receive the grant 3 years in a row. With the help of my principal, we found a way to cover any additional costs. She allowed me to handpick 20 of my top social studies students to take to the General Assembly.

WOW! is all I can say about those trips. Ohio's Statehouse was completed in 1861 just as the Civil War was beginning. The building was constructed in the Greek Revival style to symbolize the founding of democracy in Athens, Greece. It is an absolutely magnificent building, and my students were in awe as we entered the massive and ornate rotunda. During the course of the day, guides took us on a tour of the building while explaining the history and significance of the art and architecture. In addition, the students were taken to the interactive museum where they were able to explore and learn about the history of Ohio, the process for how a bill becomes a law, important men and women from Ohio and their achievements, and much more.

Perhaps the most impactful part of the day was when students were taken to the House and Senate chambers. There, staff members from the offices of our state representative and senator explained some of the processes and procedures for passing legislation. After that lesson, the students were taken to a committee room where the staff led them in a mock committee meeting. The level of engagement students had in the debate was amazing. They each were given a job and talking points to guide their individual role in the debate. The debate lasted about a half hour, and my students used the talking points, but also added their own thoughts and perspectives. This lesson was one of the most powerful I have been a part of. I'm not sure whether your statehouse offers tours like this for students, but if they do, I would highly recommend looking into ways to get your students out of the classroom for this opportunity. The value of the experience will far outweigh the expense.

What Needs to Happen

Some of my proposals may be met with criticism. That's okay. These are just my opinions. We simply can't keep arguing and playing politics with students' lives. We need to address the issues with some common sense. The following is what I believe needs to happen quickly to serve the needs of gifted students:

- **More electives.** I would like schools to consider adding more electives in the Humanities. Throughout history, these subjects have proven their value in building creativity and critical thinking skills. Schools need to offer more electives for the gifted students, or at the very minimum provide after-school clubs that are designed to challenge these kids.

- **Different track.** In some cases, we need to offer a different track (I know that is heresy to some academics and bureaucrats). I believe these students need to learn from one another and push their limits, and that can't always happen in traditional, inclusive classrooms.

- **Independent study.** I believe that many students are capable of completing independent study projects. I am proposing that schools consider offering independent study courses for students to pursue something they are passionate about. I've seen kids produce phenomenal work that has absolutely nothing to do with the curriculum I teach. Learning is learning as far as I'm concerned, and if they are learning, I'm happy.

- **Interdisciplinary units.** A collaboration among core content, arts, and technology could be used to help improve our test scores and challenge the high achievers by immersing students in content and showing relevance.

I'm sure all schools and districts are already having these conversations. Your voice matters, so be an advocate for positive change. Have discussions (not arguments) with your colleagues. Lead by example and create your own independent study or interdisciplinary unit. Don't wait until something is perfect before you roll it out. Nothing is perfect, but doing nothing is unacceptable.

Your Turn

Help your students go above and beyond.

Design a lesson for your high-achieving students that brings in at least one aspect of entrepreneurial ideas that are presented on the television show Shark Tank®. You do not need to make this a big project. It can be a simple 1-day activity that challenges your top-tier students and pushes them outside of their comfort zone.

My reflections:

_____

_____

_____

_____

_____

_____

_____

_____

_____

_____

_____

Steps to maximize my potential:

_____

_____

_____

_____

_____

_____

_____

_____

_____

_____

_____

Chapter 8

Pave the Way for Students with Special Needs

Students with impediments to learning are not getting the services they truly need in our schools (please hear me out before you freak out because I said this). The intervention specialists are heroes, but they are fighting a losing battle within an unfair system. To all my interventionist friends, you have my utmost respect. Not only do you have to find ways to help the learners who are struggling the most, but your reward is a mountain of paperwork. I want to see you get the credit you deserve. You have been dealt a lousy hand by politicians and bureaucrats.

I once had two students who had IEPs (for the layperson who may be reading this, that's Individualized Education Programs for students with some form of learning disability). These two boys definitely had trouble learning in the traditional way that we recognize school, but they displayed a level of learning that still amazes me today. Both boys were very interested in history and always were telling me about things they saw on the History Channel.

For about 8 years, I was the History Day coordinator for our school. Each year I would invite students to participate in the annual History Day competition held at the President William McKinley Presidential Library and Museum. I need to take a moment to express my sincerest gratitude for Christopher Kenny, the Director of Education at the museum that hosted the competition. He did a superb job running the program for our region and was always available to help the students and coordinators. Sadly, Chris passed too soon, and he is greatly missed. The History Day competition will never be the same without him. He made a difference in the lives of children without ever being in a classroom.

Rules and Requirements

These two boys who loved history asked whether they could participate in the competition. For those of you who aren't familiar with History Day, think of it like the Science Fair, only with about 10 times the rules and requirements. The strict entry process requires the highest academic and research standards. So there I was with two students who loved history, but definitely would struggle meeting all the necessary requirements.

The boys worked on their project with the help of many different people—among them me, their intervention specialist, their fathers and grandfathers. I can't remember exactly what the theme of History Day was that year, but the boys decided they were going to create their project on the History of the Ford Motor. The idea was very thoughtful on their part, and it aligned perfectly with the theme of the competition.

To make a long story short, getting the boys to fulfill the research, writing, annotations, works cited, yada yada yada requirements was a real struggle. I'm not saying those elements aren't important, because they are. But the requirements were a challenge for an average middle school student, let alone two who had difficulty with those aspects of academics.

The day of the competition arrived, and the boys showed up with their project. The boys were dressed in khakis (one had cowboy boots and a Ford belt buckle, the other in sneakers) and ties that clashed with the patterns on their shirts. No lie. I can't make that up. What they were wearing didn't matter to them; they were proud to be dressed up and ready to present. I greeted them and then continued to walk around to check out the other projects.

Some of the projects were awesome. They were on wooden trifolds with hinges, decorated to the hilt; one of the competitors built an actual scale model of an insane asylum that opened up like Castle Greyskull® from He-Man® so you could see the inner workings of the asylum. Unbelievable! Needless to say, her project moved on. The projects were so creative and innovative that you had no choice but to stop and find out more.

Beyond the Standards

My two guys did not have a project with all that glitz. Theirs was on poster board with cut-out letters made from construction paper and black-and-white pictures printed on the school copy machine. The poster didn't matter to them. What they were proud of was the miniature Ford motor they built. I had absolutely no idea how the judges would rank them. So we waited for the results to come in and the awards presentation to begin. Wouldn't you know it? The boys qualified to go on to the next round! They didn't score very well on the research part of the project, but their explanation and demonstration earned them a high enough score to advance to the state-level competition.

After seeing how well done the other projects were, the boys went back to create a better display and improve the research portion of their project. Unfortunately, they were eliminated in the second round. But I have to believe that this experience gave them the confidence to try harder and perform better. I'm not sure what happened to those two boys, but I will always remember the two kids who learned in their own way— above and beyond what the standards tell us to teach—to prove that learning happens in a thousand different ways.

Different Learning Options

There are so many different types of learning impediments, from SLD to ED, ASD, ELL, and on and on and on. The list seems endless. The educational system requires interventionists and general education teachers to keep track of all the modifications, develop differentiated lessons, find reading passages at the appropriate levels, accommodate schedules, develop and use RtI, and so much more. These kids have huge roadblocks to learning put in front of them, and our interventionists and classroom teachers are doing their level best.

I wonder whether our system is truly designed to help struggling learners or to make everyone learn at the same speed. Have we forgotten that we are all different? Sometimes these students just need a different learning environment or different options for what they learn and how they show what they've learned. We have to reexamine special education in our system.

In my opinion, the current system is unfair to our students. If you put me in calculus or organic chemistry or some high-level class, I can promise you that I would probably shut down the moment I lost understanding of the material. I would love to say that I would pull myself up by my bootstraps and work extra hard or extra long until I learned it, but that would be a lie. You could give me extended time, small-group instruction, read the tests to me and let me use my notes during them, and I still wouldn't have a clue. And I've always been pretty good at learning, but sometimes, the material is just above our level at a particular time. That doesn't mean we can't learn it eventually. It just means we aren't ready yet. My reaction to this situation would probably be one of the following:

- I'm hiding in the back row to make sure nobody sees me.
- I'm definitely not raising my hand to ask a question for fear that everybody knows what is going on and I am going to look stupid.
- If I'm feeling somewhat comfortable in the class, I might crack a joke or two to make people laugh so they will at least think I'm funny when they find out how clueless I am.

Does this sound familiar? That's exactly what it is like for many of these kids. Of course they don't want to try for fear of looking stupid. Yet, we continue to include them in every class, write up a list of accommodations, and assume they will learn because they are with their peers. Presumably, their peers will model the learning techniques for them or help them learn the material. In reality, the peers do all the work, and the kids who struggle watch and get credit, even though they don't learn much or anything at all.

Once kids have surpassed their frustration point, they have decided what they are going to do to avoid looking dumb. Why are we asking them to try to learn something they aren't ready for just for the sake of inclusion? Don't get me wrong; inclusion can be a good thing if it is done right. I believe it is the best thing for most kids, but not all kids.

Smart About Different Things

We need different options for these kids. Just as I suggested for gifted students, kids with special needs should have special electives—on things they are going to actually use—to prepare them for the real world. I believe that these students also should be offered independent study projects. Giving them something to learn about that they are interested in will help knock down some of the roadblocks. These students may not create the perfect quality project, but they can learn and they can show us what they learned. Period! I also believe that interdisciplinary units are great for these types of learners. They may struggle in one area, but excel in another. Interdisciplinary units allow them to put their knowledge to work in all their classes. They can feel valuable in every content area, even if they struggle with that particular content. This approach builds self-worth, resilience, and hopefully a self-realization that they can learn. They just learn in different ways or about different things.

I always tell my students that nobody knows everything. That's impossible, so we have to accept that there are just some things we won't understand. We are all smart. We are just smart about different things. I know there are things my students could teach me, just like there are things I can teach them. My students tend to feel more at ease when I say this at the beginning of the year. I refer back to it frequently when kids are struggling with something or they answer a question wrong and the class laughs. That drives me nuts, by the way, so I remind my students that nobody knows everything. Some things we just haven't learned yet. This little reminder usually quiets down the class pretty quickly. Sometimes the students even feel bad for laughing.

Your Turn

Help your students develop skills they are good at.

Have conversations with your struggling learners and try to find out something they see themselves as good at. Design a lesson for them that incorporates some of the skills they are confident in. You do not need to make this a big project. It can be a simple 1-day activity that helps your struggling students find success and value in what you teach.

My reflections:

_____

_____

_____

_____

_____

_____

_____

_____

_____

_____

_____

Steps to maximize my potential:

_____

_____

_____

_____

_____

_____

_____

_____

_____

_____

Chapter 9

Develop Relationships with Difficult Students

I don't have all the answers; I'm sorry. However, if you skipped over Chapter 3, maybe turn back and explore something that may help you unwind after days you encounter a difficult student and come home stressed. I want to tell a quick little story that reminded me that all students have good in them—even the most challenging ones. I had a group of boys one year that formed their own preteenager gang. I don't mean a street gang, but the type of gang that is going to disrupt the school environment.

Anyway, one day I lost my cool and yelled at these kids pretty harshly. After I cooled down and realized what I had done, I decided that I needed to apologize. So, during my planning period, I pulled each of these students from class. (Just a side note, if you are wondering, yes I did pull them out of other classes.) I took the boys to the gym to apologize for losing my cool, and I explained why their choices made me angry. They seemed to understand and even apologized to me. Then we shot hoops and played the basketball game knockout for 15 to 20 minutes.

A few weeks later, I got a text from a colleague letting me know that "J" just found out I wouldn't be returning to the classroom for the remainder of the year. (I had to take medical leave.) "J" told my colleague that he was mad at me for not coming back the rest of the year. He ranted about it for 10 minutes.

A Tough Nut

"J" is a very, very tough nut to crack. I'm not going to share his story, but believe me when I tell you, you wouldn't wish his childhood on your worst enemy. It is ugly and heartbreaking. "J" and I had our run-ins, and they always ended with him storming out of the classroom. His situation is bad. So as you can imagine, on the day I lost my cool, "J" was one of the boys in the gang.

After I apologized and shot hoops with the boys, the relationship changed. We were both in the wrong, and we both knew it. Apologizing, explaining, and showing that I cared about him made all the difference in my classroom. That's not to say that we didn't have our problems after that, but he didn't storm out of my room again. He sometimes needed some time to compose himself in the hall, but he always came back in.

What Has to Change

"J" had some issues that I couldn't fix. He needed help, but the system we work in doesn't have the answers either. He and thousands, perhaps tens of thousands, of students in our country are not getting the help they need. This absolutely has to change! "J," as well as all kids, have good in them. We just have to help them find it within themselves.

Based on my own observations, difficult students act out for five main reasons:

- They have experienced or are experiencing trauma.
- They are stressed.
- They crave peer approval because they don't know how to make or keep friends or need attention.
- They have a chemical imbalance.
- Their family norms are unhealthy.

When working with challenging students, keep these five possible explanations in mind and try to come up with the best possible plan for helping them. Be open to suggestions. Without question, nothing will change for them until they feel valued. Relationships matter!

Your Turn

Help your students value themselves.

Reach out to one or more of your challenging students to help them find value in themselves. As I mentioned earlier, I do not have all the answers. Teachers and others are going to have to work together to figure this out. However, I do have a couple suggestions for you to consider:

- Have a conversation with one or two of your moderately challenging students and try to find out something they see themselves as good at. Design a lesson for each student that incorporates some of the skills they are confident in. You do not need to make this a big project. It can be a simple 1-day activity that helps a particular student find success and value in what you teach.

- Ask them a question in the lesson that you know they will get correct and give them positive reinforcement.

- Point out a positive behavior they demonstrated and reinforce the heck out of it.

- Find a task or job for them to do in class that day.

- Go to their sporting event or performance and find something you can use to help them understand their value.

- Rethink how you talk about being proud of an accomplishment. Try saying, "You should be very proud of yourself!" That suggests they should see themselves in a positive way. When we say, "I am proud of you!" it makes them crave affirmation rather than increase their self-efficacy.

- Talk to a colleague and see whether they have any ideas or suggestions.

- Just listen to the students. You might be surprised what you can find out.

My reflections:

_____

_____

_____

_____

_____

_____

_____

_____

_____

_____

_____

Steps to maximize my potential:

_____

_____

_____

_____

_____

_____

_____

_____

_____

_____

Chapter 10

Teach Students to Be Proud Citizens

I've often wondered whether our nation is being hypocritical by requiring immigrants to pass a citizenship test when many of our own students, and population for that matter, wouldn't be able to pass the same test. Take a practice test to see how you would do.[2] The educational system in our country has fallen short in teaching citizenship. And our society has lost sight of how citizenship transcends politics. Both Ronald Reagan and John F. Kennedy, one a Republican and the other a Democrat, understood the importance of citizenship and pushed for it in their agendas.

---

[2] https://civicsquestions.com/all

Taking a Trip to Our Capital

For the past 6 years, I have chaperoned the eighth-grade trip to Gettysburg, and to Washington, DC. I love our nation's capital and could go back there every year for the rest of my career. Even though we see the same sights every time, I never fail to learn something new. A few of you reading this might be thinking that chaperoning a trip like this sounds awful—accompanying a bunch of eighth graders out in public where everyone knows you are responsible when they make terrible choices. I assure you that in the 6 years I have gone, some little issues have arisen; but by and large, the students are better behaved on the trip than they are in my classroom.

For many of them, this is their first taste of independence, maybe their first time leaving home for an extended time without family around. They love it and the freedom it provides. They don't want to mess that up by getting into trouble. Even some of the challenging kids will fall in line because they are surrounded by positive influences who use their peer pressure to keep others from making bad choices.

Since I have been chaperoning the trip, I have witnessed firsthand the value of taking education outside of the classroom walls.   In my experience, students who have gone on the Washington trip, if they paid the least bit of attention, developed a better understanding of our history, government, and ideals. Not all of them did, unfortunately; but for those who took in this firsthand experience, that knowledge stuck with them. Hopefully it will come back to them in the classroom or society in general when they need it.

Learning Beyond the Classroom

I have always hated that we can't afford to take every student on a trip like this. The trip doesn't have to be a big one to Washington, DC. Your local communities and states have countless places that could provide the same learning. We have to broaden students' horizons if we are going to make them lifelong learners. We can't continue to box ourselves into learning within four walls or on a screen. That isn't the real world. Distance and remote learning can be a very small part of that learning, but are not a substitute for the actual experience.

Please do not take this as boasting or tooting my own horn, but I want to share one of the things I am most proud of as an educator. I just mentioned that I hate that we can't afford to take every student on a trip. Over the past 6 years, I have paid for four students to go on the Washington trip out of my pocket. Again, please don't judge me; I just couldn't stand the idea that these kids couldn't go on the trip because their families couldn't afford it. That is so wrong in so many ways. To me, it's just money. I will make more. These kids needed this trip. They never knew who paid for it, only that an anonymous donor provided funds and they were chosen to go.

I made sure that each year, the student I paid for was in my group, and I gave that student $40 to spend. All the students I sponsored formed friendships, had some laughs, and hopefully learned a thing or two on the trip. In my mind, the price was a small way that I could help. I am fully aware that many teachers do similar things all the time, perhaps even more. I mention this only because it made me feel good to know that I could help others. That's all.

Celebrating Our History

We have not taught our students to be proud of their country. Yes, we have committed atrocities, and sure we have made countless mistakes; but our nation has been a world leader in creativity, innovation, technology, athletics, entertainment, medicine, and science for years. Why don't we celebrate that? We have to teach all the history of our society—the good, the bad, and unfortunately the awful. That is how we learn from our mistakes. And we also should celebrate our greatness. Everyone wants to feel valued, and we can feel proud as a country if we celebrate our successes.

We need to teach our kids what being a citizen of this country means. You may disagree with our nation's history, policies, or politics, but remember that our society functions only when the people put disagreement aside in the interest of helping others. Change needs to happen in our society, but it has to be change that is fair for all people. That's what our students need to understand. We need to challenge their thought process and sometimes play devil's advocate. However, before we can do that, they need an accurate education on the history of our country and the world. They need to see that humans have tried a lot of things in the past. Some worked, some didn't, but we can't go back and make the same mistakes people have been making for millennia.

Giving Back

I believe that our students need to understand the importance of giving back to their neighborhoods, communities, states, and country. This country provides millions of us with the opportunities to find what fulfills us. Even as bad off as some folks are, our country still works to help them through government assistance, charity, and job opportunities if they want them.

Enjoying Freedoms

Once again, I want to state for the record that I know we are not perfect, our society isn't fair for everyone, but I don't see too many people lining up to leave America. I do, however, see a lot trying to come here. That is a testament to the greatness of America. We are the only country on Earth that was built out of the greatness of all the other cultures on the planet. That we became the envy of the world is not an accident. Immigrants to the United States see themselves in us and want the freedoms we enjoy. People from around the world want to come here for the opportunities we provide. We should celebrate our multiculturalism. Our ancestors were all immigrants at one point, and they brought their wonderful culture with them to share in America. Our society is truly a melting pot. That should be celebrated, taught, and we should continue to work to make it better and more fair.

Knowing Our History

Understanding our history and being proud of America is essential to our success. Some bad actors in the world would like nothing more than to see our experiment with freedom and democracy fail. They contend that humans are meant to be ruled as we have been for millennia. When did patriotism become something we should be ashamed of? None of us can fix our past; we can only learn from our mistakes and commit to doing better next time. That's one of the ways we, as humans, learn. As much as we would like to erase all the horrific parts of our history, that is not how our society will learn and grow. We absolutely must know our history, or we will be blindsided by another horrific event. We have to keep improving!

Your Turn

Help your students celebrate their citizenship.

Design and teach a lesson that celebrates anything about the American spirit. You do not need to make this a big project; it can be a 1-day lesson.

Here are a few ideas to get you thinking about your lesson:

- Identify a person who exhibited tremendous service or sacrifice to America.
- Select someone who prevailed over injustice, discrimination, prejudice, and racism.
- Choose an American innovation that changed the world for the better.
- Pick out some great American achievements in the subject area you teach (e.g., sports, performance or visual arts, science, technology, math, social studies, writing, entrepreneurship).

My reflections:

_____
_____
_____
_____
_____
_____
_____
_____
_____
_____
_____
_____

Steps to maximize my potential:

_____
_____
_____
_____
_____
_____
_____
_____
_____
_____
_____
_____

PART IV:

EFFECTING CHANGE

Chapter 11

Instill a Love of Learning

I'm not an expert. I don't have a PhD or EdD. My research has come through my experiences as a classroom teacher for 23 years. These are just thoughts and opinions for your consideration. Nobody has all the right answers, certainly not me; but until we start asking the right questions and considering different ideas, we are going to be stuck spinning our wheels.

It's time to take a little break from reading. You can come back to the book later if you want. I would like to ask you to try something. You may see this as a waste of time, but then again, you may find it cathartic. Make a list of everything that is wrong with education. Not a mental list; write down an actual list. Take as much time as you need. Putting together your list might take you a couple minutes, or you might still be working on it a month from now. It doesn't really matter how long it takes. This may seem like a negative thing to do, but I believe that by identifying problems, we begin the process of solving them.

Journaling

I always saw my career taking the following path: teacher and coach, then principal, and then maybe a district office role. I never wanted to be a superintendent, but maybe something in curriculum or operations would be my final role before retirement. This seemed like the logical progression. Life usually has different plans for us, and to this point in time, I have been only a teacher and coach. I have had some teacher leadership roles, but I have never been in charge of a building.

Since my first year of teaching, I have kept a very informal journal of my thoughts, experiences, observations, and beliefs about education. When I say an "informal" journal, I mean that I write thoughts on scraps of paper, in notebooks, on legal pads, and in documents on my computer. I keep these notes because I plan to use them as my guide if and when I become a principal. Without realizing it, I have basically been building my core set of beliefs and values that would guide me when I didn't know what to do as a principal. Everyone should have a core set of beliefs and values to rely on when you don't have the answer to a tough situation.

I suppose this is why I am asking you to make a list of everything that is wrong with education. By identifying what is wrong, and not just talking about it but writing it down, you automatically will begin the process of trying to figure out how to fix it. In the process of coming up with your solutions, you will begin identifying your core values because your solution to the problem is ultimately what you believe is right. Maybe you find value in this little activity, maybe not. Journaling is something that helps me stay grounded when everything in education seems to be flipping upside down.

Expanding Our Focus

In my opinion, our number one job is to foster a love of learning that will carry throughout the lifetime of our students. If they love learning, they can learn whatever they need to know to be successful in their future career. I fear that we are focusing only on Math and English/Language Arts (ELA), with a minor focus on science and technology. Those courses, while extremely important, are not necessarily going to determine success in life. We need to help our students become more well-rounded, not less. We need to provide more opportunities for kids, not fewer. We need to encourage them to try more things to see what they like, or enjoy, or feel good about. Hopefully they will find their passion; if they do, they will be fulfilled in life. At the bare minimum, they should at least be able to find what makes them happy and satisfied.

Our focus should be on rich educational opportunities in all academic content areas, including science and technology, social sciences, the trades, and the arts. We should not continue to try to make kids into something they are not. We are all different learners with different talents, likes, and dislikes. Why do we continue to say that everybody needs to excel in Math and ELA when life will take our students down so many other avenues?

I'm not saying we shouldn't do everything in our power to help them improve in Math and ELA, but these are not the be all and end all.

Identifying the Nonnegotiable

Not only is it our responsibility to instill a love of learning, but we also must develop in our students a strong work ethic and pride in citizenship. I wonder whether we are doing that. More and more we hear from universities and the business world that students lack the soft skills necessary to be successful. What can we do to improve that? I would argue that schools need to have a set of non-negotiable values to exemplify the importance of guidance through complicated decisions.

Examples of what that would look like:

- We do the right thing.
- We are responsible for our own success.
- We come to school on time and prepared to learn.
- We are polite and respectful.
- We meet deadlines and due dates.
- We give our best in everything we do.
- We think "yes" not "no."
- We all help one another.
- We always try.
- We aim high.
- We stay positive and productive.

- We have faith in ourselves.
- We always keep our word.

Brainstorming Solutions

I believe we are at a turning point in education. Some of the proposals I am presenting should be met with skepticism. They may be expensive. Some may even sound ridiculous to you. However, the time is ripe for thoughtful and maybe even drastic change. So here are some of the things I believe we should consider.

Teaching Assistants

Every teacher should have an assistant, just like all doctors have nurses, lawyers have paralegals, and businesspeople have office assistants. I propose that universities begin creating an associate's degree for teacher assistants. Think of the role as similar to a veterinary technician or dental hygienist. They are not specialists, but they are knowledgeable and trained to help the specialist. We need help in the classroom to work with all the different styles of learners and all the different challenges they bring. One person in the classroom is just not enough anymore. Furthermore, I believe that each grade-level content area, including specials and electives, should have a dedicated intervention specialist. Co-teaching will improve the capacity for learning because the interventionists will be more immersed in the content and not spread too thin.

Humanities

Many schools do not have enough enrichment courses available for the Humanities. The Humanities (Language, Social Sciences, Philosophy, the Arts) build great critical thinking skills and creativity. Unfortunately, this deficiency is a result of the unfair funding systems. Schools with large populations in high socioeconomic areas can offer these courses, while schools with small populations in poor or rural areas cannot. Unfair! I'm not talking about just giving students some online learning program to do on their own; this enrichment should be offered by schools with trained teachers.

Interdisciplinary Units

I believe that we should start to focus on interdisciplinary units involving core content, arts, and technology. As long as testing is still a thing, this strategy could help improve our test scores by immersing students in content and showing its relevance across curricula. The more students see or hear the same information across curricula, the more likely they are to remember it and be able to apply it when necessary.

More importantly, however, is that we should use interdisciplinary units to prepare our students for the challenges of life. We don't live in a vacuum where we need only this information for this or that information for that. Life doesn't work that way. We have things coming at us from all different directions, and we have to use our knowledge and experiences and instincts to help us navigate life. Yet when I think about school, we have created a system where kids live in the ELA vacuum or the Math vacuum or in whatever content vacuum is being taught in the classroom. I know that we bring aspects of other content into our classrooms, but the primary focus is on the single content area that is supposed to be taught in that class. Unfortunately, that doesn't align with the reality of how the world works.

We should be incorporating more interdisciplinary units in classrooms to prepare our kids for the world they will be working and living in as adults. They need to see how all the information they are learning is tied together and can be used in more than just the classroom.

Team Teaching

If we really want to take this to the next level, we could consider allowing teams of teachers to take all the grade-level content standards and divide them up among themselves. This might work only in the primary and middle grade levels due to the nature and complexity of content at higher grade levels. However, I think this approach could serve younger learners well.

Here is my vision:

- We are all teachers of content (including interventionists, art, music, physical education, tech, etc.), but we are also knowledgeable, experienced people in society. We are capable of teaching more than one thing well.

- We all have skills, talents, and interests. As a social studies teacher, I have a passion for history, but I also love reading and art and music. If I feel comfortable teaching some of those things, then I believe I should be able to teach them. Passion for the subject or a particular area of the subject will help teachers be more effective.

- Many times in my career, I have been asked to teach something I wasn't interested in. I did my best, but I didn't bring the energy or excitement to the lesson, and the kids saw that. They almost always are more engaged in the lessons I am passionate about.

- Not everything will be exciting for the kids; but when the teacher is excited, they tend to be more excited. Passion is contagious.

- If other teachers in my grade level are passionate about something that I'm not in my content area, why wouldn't I hand that over to them to teach and vice versa?

Kids will see teachers as more than just specialists in one content area. Hopefully they will see that learning is holistic and that all content has value in their lives. I believe this approach models the benefits of being well-rounded and lifelong learners and allows students to see their teachers demonstrating this virtue.

You would still be the primary instructor in your content; but if someone can teach it better, then they should. In my opinion, this strategy would help keep teaching fresh because teachers would be researching and teaching what we are passionate about. Furthermore, this approach may reduce burnout and complacency. Who wouldn't want to teach their passion?

Why will this idea be met with opposition? TESTING! No teachers want to give up control of their content when their evaluation is tied to testing results. Once again, I want to reiterate how testing brings stress to the workplace. Giving up control when your name is on the report card is scary, and we all know how fear prevents change. But I believe that this simple change can help improve learning throughout all our schools.

Another hurdle will be the teaming of teachers. You have to trust your colleagues, and they have to trust you. If teachers aren't teamed properly, this idea will never work. We all perceive the ineffective teachers in our buildings, and nobody will trust them to teach "their" content. However, this strategy could be the catalyst for ineffective teachers to become better. When they are teaching things they enjoy and others are counting on them, they will step up their game. If not, then it is time for them to go.

This may seem ridiculous, but what if kids didn't go to Social Studies class, but instead went to Mr. Eibel's class to learn what he is teaching that day? This idea is even a little out there for me, but I think it should be considered and discussed critically. It might be just what we need. I know this would take an enormous amount of planning; but once it is done, teachers should have to make only minor adjustments or tweaks to their units each year based on their reflection on the lessons.

Degrees of effectiveness vary in all professions. Some people are more talented than others. Some work harder than others. We need staff who are reliable, work hard, reflect on their practice, and try to improve each and every day. I cannot accept anything less than that. When we have staff who are not meeting that standard, then we need to help them or sometimes make tough choices. Staff morale suffers when people perceive paid employees not pulling their own weight. We don't need to be cruel, but we must hold them accountable for getting better at their job. Teachers who are passionate aren't always effective, but teachers who aren't passionate are almost never effective.

Changing the Schedule

Perhaps the biggest change I am proposing is a 4-day school week spread out over a longer period of time. I believe this will lead to higher levels of retention and less burnout and frustration. Let me start by saying that *I am not* advocating for a longer school day. Rather, we could spread out the 185 school days over more of the calendar year.

The story of how I stumbled on the 4-day calendar idea began in September of the 2021–2022 school year. I couldn't stand seeing how stressed my colleagues were, and we hadn't even been in school for a month. How could they possibly be that stressed out already? Usually that level of stress doesn't set in until January. I just couldn't help but wonder whether we could do something to alleviate the stress that everyone was under. It was killing us, or at least making us miserable.

The idea for the 4-day week spread out over more of the year was an idea I came up wIth (I know that examples of this are already out there; it isn't new). I shouldn't say I came up with it; it just dawned on me that maybe we should take a look at the 4-day work schedule. Everybody loves a 4-day work week. You're already excited at the beginning of each week because you know that you only have to work 4 days. It might have even been a 4-day week when I had this epiphany. I'm not really sure of the exact day or week, but let's just call it a 4-day week for the sake of levity.

Anyway, I printed off some yearly calendars for next school year and started filling in the days for school with periodic breaks in the fall, winter, and spring (see Appendix D). What I found is that if you start the school year in June—wait, that's going to blow everyone's mind, but hear me out— and end at Memorial Day, you have the framework for year-round school.

By starting in June, you actually are giving teachers and students a full year in which to teach and learn the curriculum before the dreaded testing that begins around the beginning of April and finishes in May. Not to mention, there are very few administrators, teachers, or students who like school in the month of May anyway, because for most students, when the test is over, school is over. May is usually when many schools see the majority of their behavior problems. By starting school in June, school never really ends, so we might not see as many behavior problems as we currently do. The learning can just continue uninterrupted into the next grade.

Students and staff would still have breaks. I believe that the breaks would allow for more periodic rest and relaxation (stress relief), possible vacations in off-peak pricing seasons, which would save teachers and the families of our students a bunch of money, not to mention more flexibility to schedule vacations so their kids don't have to miss school because of their own issues with getting off work. Most importantly, and really the only reason that matters, year-round learning would help kids retain the knowledge we want them to retain.

My proposal would still be a 185-day calendar for teachers, which means the change would not hit the pocketbooks of the taxpayers; and with the funding to build schools across the states and country, many buildings are now equipped with higher-efficiency heating and cooling systems. No more using the excuse, "They can't go to school in the summer; it's too hot."

I met with my superintendent to talk about some of the issues and ideas I had, and he couldn't have been more welcoming and appreciative. He didn't even look at me like I had three eyes when I talked to him about this idea. He seemed very supportive of the idea, but obviously this is a logistics nightmare. Just take a look at the two versions of a yearly calendar I included in Appendix D. Maybe I am crazy? You decide.

IMPROVING YOUR TEACHING

Just some odds and ends for you to think about.

These have all helped me improve as an individual teacher:

- Teachers who ask students to do things rather than tell students to do something tend to find that strategy to be more effective.
- Be kind and treat others the way we want to be treated, including students. It's a phrase that has stood the test of time, and it is universal in the teachings of other cultures and religions.
- Help kids find some success and celebrate it when they do. They will start to believe they can learn, and their effort will improve.
- Use the word *practice* instead of the word *study*. I believe that the more we practice something, the

better we get at that task. Therefore, I ask students to "practice" their vocabulary words or "practice" for their test. Practice sounds easier than study because I relate it to sports, music, video games, and other activities.

I want to leave you with one final task. I'm sorry—I know you didn't think you would have homework. What would you do to become a better teacher if you had a semester sabbatical? Make a list of all the things you would do during that semester that would help you be the best version of your teaching self when you return. Maybe we can convince the powers that be that sabbaticals should be offered in our contracts.

Your Turn

State the problems as the first step toward finding solutions.

Make a list of all the things wrong with the educational system. By identifying what is wrong, and not just talking about it, but writing it down, you will automatically begin the process of trying to figure out how to fix it. In the process of coming up with your solutions, you will begin identifying your core values because your solution to the problem is ultimately what you believe is right. Maybe you will find value in this little activity, maybe not. Journaling is something that helps me stay grounded when everything in education seems to be flipping upside down.

My reflections:

_____
_____
_____
_____
_____
_____
_____
_____
_____
_____
_____

Steps to maximize my potential:

_____
_____
_____
_____
_____
_____
_____
_____
_____
_____
_____

Chapter 12

Be the Best Teacher You Can Be

This is a chapter that I considered calling "Tough Love." It's not what we all want to hear, but sometimes it is something we need to hear. I'm sure this is going to ruffle some feathers, but I feel it must be said. I am addressing one of the many elephants in the room, so here goes.

The Power to Non-Renew

Administration should have more power to non-renew teaching contracts for teachers who are not getting the job done. I know this is not a popular sentiment among many readers. You may be thinking that is too much power for one or two administrators to have, but it is necessary. Welcome to the reality of how the rest of the organizations of the world operate. Bosses fire people for poor performance.

We may be working with colleagues who aren't effective at reaching students. In my experience, the system has caused administration to move personnel around so they can "hide" the ineffective teachers. Obviously that is not a good thing. Once the personnel dominoes begin to fall, due to licensure and HQT (Highly Qualified Teachers standards), good teachers end up getting moved in order to hide the less effective teachers. This is terrible for staff morale because they see a "bad" teacher getting what they perceive to be a gravy gig.

It's worse for the teachers who get moved. They are stuck wondering why they are getting punished for someone else not doing their job. The bottom line: These teachers aren't good for kids. If you can look at yourself in the mirror and know that you are doing the best you can, you have nothing to worry about. However, if you aren't getting the job done, maybe some other profession would suit you better.

I mentioned this anecdote in an earlier chapter, but I think it is worth reiterating. My situation didn't involve a bad teacher getting "hidden," but it did show how the system can be bad for morale. My story happened 3 years ago. While the administration was planning for the upcoming school year, the staffing dominoes began to fall. Unfortunately, I was blindsided by a sudden change.

Due to licensure, HQT, and all that bureaucracy, a high school teacher needed to be moved down to seventh-grade social studies, and I was reassigned to sixth-grade social studies. At least I was still in the content area I enjoy (which is more than I can say for some teachers who get reassigned), but I was no longer in my dream job. I hold no animosity whatsoever toward the teacher who replaced me in seventh grade. She is a wonderful person. However, we were both victims of the bureaucracy and put into positions that may not have been best for either of us.

What's Best for Students

Administration was just doing what was necessary to be good stewards of the taxpayers' money. Schools should be fiscally conscientious, but money shouldn't be the driving force in the quality of education our students receive. Licensure and HQT are important, but they don't take into account a teacher's natural ability. They assume that teachers can teach in only one or two areas.

In my opinion, that is an absurd way of thinking. I'm pretty confident that a doctor trained in oncology could probably also treat me for the flu. Teachers can absolutely do the same thing. Just because we have more training in one area doesn't mean we aren't capable of teaching something else. I would like for politicians and bureaucrats to take a critical look at licensure and HQT and ask themselves whether this is what is really best for students. I'm certain that some will say that it is absolutely what's best, but others might see that we are really limiting the experiences students have in school by tying their teachers' hands.

Get the Job Done

Here is the hard truth for teachers who aren't getting the job done; it might be time for a change. Maybe the change is as simple as a new assignment, a new building or district. If you really aren't enjoying what you do, you may want to consider a new career. This job is much too important for teachers who just go through the motions to be in a classroom. Find something you love; if working in a tough, challenging profession isn't what you love, then you shouldn't be doing it.

Administrators, you aren't off the hook either. Everything I asserted previously applies to you as well. I propose that teachers and staff should have the ability to take a vote of no confidence in any administrators who they believe are not cut out to lead them. Once administrators have lost the support of the staff, they are lame ducks. Schools cannot run efficiently if the staff and administration don't trust or work well with one another. We can't let poor leaders continue to run buildings, and worse yet, we shouldn't waste taxpayers' money trying to hide them in gravy administration jobs. It isn't fair to the staff or students. I want to reiterate that education is much too important to have bad leaders in administrative roles. Imagine having one ineffective teacher ruining a class for all the students they interact with. Even

135

worse is to have an ineffective administrator making the job for his or her staff even more difficult. That affects literally hundreds or thousands of kids each year.

SWAPPING ROLES

I propose that all administrators spend a semester each licensing period in a regular teaching setting. During this time, I believe it would be valuable for administrators to swap roles with teachers who are prospective administrators. Obviously a prospective administrator wouldn't be able to just completely take over the job, so I see the relationship as more of a partnership. If done properly, this would be a natural learning experience for both people involved. With the help of the teacher, an administrator would teach his or her class and everything involved with that.

Reciprocally, the administrator would help the prospect manage that new role. Administrators would begin to understand everything that they are asking of teachers. On the other hand, prospective administrators would get training and experiences to help them decide whether they really want to pursue a leadership role.

Each party needs to truly understand what the other is being asked to do. The only way to do that is by doing it. Of course there has to be accountability; and of course we need to protect teachers and administrators from harassment or unfair termination, but removing staff that isn't good for kids has gotten way too difficult.

My thoughts on leadership are as follows:

- Have a vision.
- Trust your conscience.
- Do what is right.
- Respect different opinions.
- Listen.
- Stay organized.
- Lead by example.

Enough said.

Your Turn

Hold yourself accountable.

Accountability works only when we hold ourselves accountable first. Find some time to reflect on your professional life. Think about an aspect of your career in which you would like to improve. Make a conscious choice to hold yourself accountable for that one area in which you would like to improve. It might be something like arriving at work 10 minutes early because you always feel rushed and stressed when you arrive. It could be more complex such as making positive phone calls to students' parents or guardians each day. What you choose really doesn't matter; just make a conscious effort to hold yourself accountable.

My reflections:

_____
_____
_____
_____
_____
_____
_____
_____
_____
_____
_____

Steps to maximize my potential:

_____
_____
_____
_____
_____
_____
_____
_____
_____
_____
_____

Chapter 13

Shine a Positive Light

Nobody outside education wants to talk about schools in a positive light. Not politicians, not the media, not even community members. When was the last time you spoke to someone outside the profession who had something good to say about education? And I'm not talking about backhanded comments like, "Bless your heart. I could never do that."

The people I speak to about education only want to talk about how they could never do that job or how they would just go off on those kids. You also hear the talk about what this teacher did, or the media focus on this school scandal or that teacher accused of wrongdoing. The pressure to get eyes on the screen drives the media to focus on the negative stories. I will give them a little credit, though. From time to time they do put a small blurb in the newspaper, or they do a 1-minute segment about something positive happening in schools. Unfortunately, those usually are buried in the back of the paper or in one of the final segments of the news. Sadly, the ugly story gets the headlines, the front page, and the attention.

Flip the Narrative

The media often paint our profession in a negative light. It's time to flip the narrative. We need to do something so powerful that they won't have a choice but to talk about all the good things happening in education. Parents will have no choice but to talk about how much their children love school. This goal isn't out of reach. We will never be the sexy story, but we sure as hell won't be the terrible story either. One of my former principals believed strongly in this initiative. She always was asking for positive things happening in classrooms or photos of students engaged in meaningful learning. I believe she understood the power of a positive message. I thank her for opening my eyes to the importance of flooding the media with positivity. Our stories didn't always make it to press, but she sure did try.

Create a Media Strategy

I'm proposing that schools change the narrative by creating a media strategy that uses local newspapers, local TV, advertisements, a YouTube channel, email, and social media to bombard them with the outstanding things happening in schools. The effort can't be just monthly or quarterly emails or mailings. It has to be much more frequent than that. People need constant reminders about positive things. They already get enough negative news.

We can't let the media continue to dictate our story. We have to control the narrative. Otherwise we will continue to be made to look like a bunch of selfish, lazy, incompetent pedophiles. We have to do a better job of getting our successes out there.

I want to share my heartfelt thanks to LeBron James for what he is doing with his "I Promise" school. He is trying to make a difference in education. He isn't the only one, but the media get fixated on him because he is a celebrity.

The people in the building are the ones who are working to make the difference at the "I Promise" school. He gave them the platform. They are doing the work. Let's not forget that.

Thank you, Lebron, for showing that there is a different way. I truly appreciate what you are trying to do.

Your Turn

Control your messaging.

We can't control the media, but we can control our own messaging. Create a list of ways in which you feel comfortable communicating with parents. For some, it may be social media. For others, it may be email or SMS messages. Regardless of which form of communication you choose, be consistent in your messaging to parents. Try to send a class update at least once a week showing the positive and exciting things happening in your classroom. Nothing beats the power of a positive message.

My reflections:

_____
_____
_____
_____
_____
_____
_____
_____
_____
_____

Steps to maximize my potential:

_____
_____
_____
_____
_____
_____
_____
_____
_____
_____

Chapter 14

Assume a Supplemental Role

Kids often remember their coaches, band or choir directors, theater directors, club leaders, and so forth long after they graduate. In many cases these may be the only people in the school that made an impression on them. Teaching is obviously important, but there is so much more to education than just what happens between 7:00 and 3:00. So I would argue that getting involved in a supplemental role will actually be a good thing for you. It will give you the ability to make even more of a difference in the lives of your students.

Getting Creative

Some of the best teachers I have ever been around are those who coach or work in visual and performing arts. They work with kids in different settings and get to know them in different ways. For those of us who have worked with students outside the classroom walls, I truly believe that it helps us better understand how to reach kids and get them to achieve at higher levels. Coaches and directors have to get creative when figuring out how to get kids to buy into their program. Classroom teachers who coach or direct or work in supplemental positions can bring that creativity and those relationship-building techniques to their classroom.

If you have never considered a supplemental position that allows you to work with kids outside the classroom, I would highly recommend that you think about getting involved in an area that interests you. Doing so will make you a more effective teacher because it gives you more tools in your tool belt.

A Lasting Impression

From time to time I will see former students and athletes out in social settings. I remember one night I stopped at a bar to grab something to eat, and I ran into a few of my former athletes who were celebrating. I don't remember exactly what they were celebrating, but they invited me into their party. We had so much fun, maybe a little too much fun, but the point is that they certainly did not have to invite me over to their table. Maybe it was the booze; but for whatever reason, they wanted to spend time with me that evening. I'm not sure whether they ever learned anything from me. I hope that I helped them a little along the way. But that wasn't what they remembered that night. They remembered that I cared about them, and so they wanted to include me in their party.

Staying in Touch

I have numerous other examples, but the two that I am most proud of are friendships that I built with two of my former student athletes. I have kept in touch with both of them since they graduated from high school. The first one went on to Ashland University and graduated with a business degree. My wife and I went to some of his college football games, and he and I still get together for dinner whenever our schedules allow. I am very proud to call him a good friend now. He has made my life better, and I hope that I have made a little difference in his life.

Making a Difference

The second young man went to Bowling Green University and graduated with a teaching degree in comprehensive social studies. Throughout college, he would send me texts now and then to let me know how he was doing and how school was going. He also would ask for advice and suggestions for things he could do in his student teaching. One text in particular still makes me a little misty. It was the one in which he told me that I was the reason he wanted to become a social studies teacher and coach. I don't even know what to say about that except that it fills me with pride. Now to wipe away the tears and continue writing. We make a difference. PERIOD!

Your Turn

Volunteer to help.

Consider volunteering to help a sports team, music program, theatrical production, or school club. By volunteering, you have the opportunity to see your students in a different environment, while still maintaining a work–life balance.

My reflections:

_____

_____

_____

_____

_____

_____

_____

_____

_____

_____

_____

Steps to maximize my potential:

_____

_____

_____

_____

_____

_____

_____

_____

_____

_____

_____

CHAPTER 15

ADVOCATE FOR ADEQUATE AND FAIR FUNDING

Figuring out how to pay for education is never easy. Because no money for education comes from the Political Action Committees (PACs) that fund their campaigns, politicians don't care about education funding. They just want to be able to say that test scores went up under their watch, or their bill improved schools. They aren't interested in real change, so they don't find creative or fair ways to fund it.

Fair Taxes

Simply put, free public education is expensive. The needs of the students have never been greater. We must figure out a fair system to pay for the change that is needed. I am never for higher taxes, but I am for fair taxes. Increasing the state sales tax could be a start. In my opinion, that is the most fair form of taxation we have. The percentage is the same for everyone who purchases something, making it fair for all. Everyone pays the same percent in sales tax regardless of whether they are buying Crayons or a Cadillac. Sales tax is also the only optional tax we have. If you really want something, you will buy it and pay the tax. If you don't like how much the tax is, you don't have to buy the product. It is fair and optional.

This increase in the sales tax should be dedicated specifically to children's education. No more loopholes, legal jargon, or funny business that allows politicians to rob our kids' piggy banks so they can use the money somewhere else. Whatever is in the pot should be equally distributed among all children regardless of address. Whether a child grows up in a trailer or a mansion shouldn't matter; all children are valuable. Their education should be funded equally. Perhaps most importantly, the education budget must be totally transparent. The formula for this increase doesn't have to be complicated:

$ per student = total revenue from sales tax increase / total number of students

Let me reiterate that math is not my strong suit, but I see this as a pretty easy formula to use. Maybe it is more complicated than I realize, but it seems pretty straightforward to me.

Raising Additional Funds

That's not to say that individual cities, counties, or districts can't do more to raise revenue for their schools. In addition to the increase in sales tax, states should allow for what I am going to call a State Funding Plus program. Simply put, districts should know exactly how much money they are going to receive from the state. School treasurers shouldn't have to guess and build forecasts or budgets based on little to no information because the funding system is so complex or antiquated.

School districts should be permitted to ask their local taxpayers for more revenue to support additional programming. That should be left to individual districts to determine how much more their community would be willing to pay. Sure there will still be schools that are financially better off than others, but the state government will have fulfilled its responsibility to fund all children equally. There can be debate over equity vs. equality, but there can be no debate on the importance of properly funding schools.

Don't tell me that education isn't important to spend money on. It's only the future of our children, communities, states, and country. Our government wastes so much money on stupid things. You know what I'm talking about. You can't tell me investing in our children is a waste of money. It is the one resource we have to ensure that America stays one of the greatest countries the world has ever known.

Your Turn

Help your school district.

Contact your state elected representatives and ask them to adequately and fairly fund public education in your state. They all have email contact forms. You don't have to be loud; but if we have enough voices, the volume will increase.

My reflections:

_____

_____

_____

_____

_____

_____

_____

_____

_____

_____

_____

Steps to maximize my potential:

_____

_____

_____

_____

_____

_____

_____

_____

_____

_____

Chapter 16

Closing Thoughts

Sometimes I feel like a silent war is waging between teachers and administration. The divide is unspoken in public, but certainly is discussed behind closed doors. Both sides are stuck between a rock and a hard place. Administrators have to do just what their name implies: administer board policy and adhere to state and federal laws. They don't necessarily agree with the policies, but they have to enforce them.

Teachers, on the other hand, don't always understand the policies and laws. They perceive the administration as forcing yet another thing on them when the problem isn't the administration at all. Actually, some politician or bureaucrat just developed this new "must do" as the silver bullet to solve all our problems. This seeming rift is causing stress on both sides. And when stress levels rise, the students suffer the consequences. The situation is so terribly sad for everyone involved.

If the politicians and bureaucrats won't help us, then we need to help ourselves. We can still do what is legally required, but we can do it in a better way. Positive press, which is difficult to get, and constituent pressure may be the only things that influence politicians to change (we certainly don't have the money to influence policy). But we can't wait for that to happen! We must begin to make the necessary changes in our own classrooms, in our buildings, and in our districts. Serving our students is too important to wait any longer. I'm willing to do it. Are you?

I'm certainly not done with education. I'm just getting started. I will practice what I preach to help make the system work better for our students. I invite you to join me.

EPILOGUE

THINK ABOUT IT

Think about one last scenario. For those of you who are parents, ask yourself these questions: What type of classroom do I want my children in? What opportunities do I want my children to have? Even if you don't have children, stand in the shoes of a parent you know for a few minutes.

Now imagine that your child has a learning disability, is gifted, has trouble making friends, is on the spectrum, or has a chemical imbalance that causes the child to be impulsive or make bad choices. What would you do to make sure your own child had all the support needed to be successful? We have to treat all children like our own. I know that they aren't, but put yourself in the shoes of the parents. They want the best for their kids, and making sure that happens is up to us. Parenting doesn't come with a training manual. We know what we know, and we parent like we were parented. For many of us, we had loving, supportive, families that valued education. That's probably why we chose this profession.

Of course, not everyone is raised in a loving family. You may be looking back at your childhood thinking, "I did this all on my own." Regardless of how you were raised, you likely remember people along the way who cared about you, helped you, and supported you. Maybe among them were family members, friends, coaches, and probably even a teacher or two who took an interest in you. What would your life look like if you hadn't had that love and support along the way? Would you be where you're at? These questions are tough to answer because we don't get a do-over. We can't fix the past.

All I'm asking you to do is think about those who helped you and come to your own conclusion. Should we indeed treat all children as if they are our own? Maybe you are pretty sure that your child would never get into trouble. And maybe you think that parents don't even care anymore. If I got in trouble at school, I could count on double trouble at home. We can't control parents, but we definitely can control how we treat their children.

Find the good in all kids. It's there; we just need to unmask it and pull it out of them. You would expect that from your child's teacher, and you probably wouldn't settle for less. Working with kids who are needy, or who are struggling learners, or who exhibit challenging behaviors is tough. Would you just throw your hands up and say "not my problem" if it was your child? Would you be thinking, "I shouldn't have to deal with this. Let someone else handle it"? I bet you would find your child the needed help. People aren't perfect, and there are no perfect families. What would you do if it were your child? As their teacher, you have the power to make sure that every child gets treated fairly. You can make that happen!

ACKNOWLEDGMENTS

To my wife Amy—I try each day to make sure she knows how much I appreciate her.

To my parents—I truly don't have the words to speak about the importance of my parents, so I will just leave it there. I just want them to know that I have felt their love and support every second of my life, and I am eternally grateful that they are my parents.

To Terry and Jan Szwast—for giving me their blessing to marry their only child. They put their faith in me to take care of her, and I try to make them proud every day.

To my sister Cara —I wasn't the best brother growing up, and it is the greatest regret of my life. I am so happy that we have grown closer over these past years. And more importantly, I am so happy you found Bryan. You two complete each other, and I look forward to making so many more memories with the two of you.

To my cousins Tom and Jim Eibel and Matt Malavite—for being the brothers I never had.

To Pete Kandis, Nick Stepanovich, Derek Faiello, Rocco Serafini, and Rich Hussar—Your friendship means the world to me. Thank you for always being there for me, never judging me, and lifting me up when I was at some of the lowest points of my life.

To Gust and Patsy Malavite—for all your love, support, guidance, and wisdom.

To Zanna Feitler—my TM teacher. She opened my eyes by literally teaching me how to close them.

To Michele Pedone—for showing me what it takes to become a great teacher. I never achieved this status, but thanks to her, I know it when I see it. She is just one of many who have been unfairly assigned because of our system of testing; forced to teach ELA because she is so good when her real passion is social studies, a non-tested subject in middle school in Ohio. It's unfair.

To Tim and Gay Welker—who in many ways helped shape my philosophies and beliefs.

To Kathie-Jo Arnoff and Lynette Greenfield - without their expertise, you most certainly would not be reading this book. They made this possible.

To all the readers—for your time and willingness to think critically about the direction of education. You are heroes.

Nobody reads the Acknowledgments in a book, but obviously you did. Thank you for that. I really do appreciate it. Email me at teacherscansaveteachers@gmail.com and I will send the first 100 people a gift card to reimburse you for the cost of the book, and as my way of seeing whether you read all the way to the end. Just a little teacher trick a lot of us know about, but I thought it might be a nice way for you to end your read.

Appendix A

Try Meditation

According to Maharishi Mahesh Yogi, the man who brought Transcendental Meditation™ (TM) into the mainstream, "Teaching is a natural profession for humans." He goes on to say that we are always teaching and showing others how to do things: "Anyone who has any knowledge can't feel rested until he has given it out." I believe this is a profound and true statement.

Transcendental Meditation is not a religion. It is not a philosophy. It is a technique that helps the brain to go inward, toward the center, where peace and calm reside. Practicing TM is like plugging yourself in to get the energy you need to live to your full capacity. As our mental, social, emotional, and physical batteries drain, TM provides us with an opportunity to recharge— something we need to do often as teachers.

Does It Work?

You should be skeptical. You should question. You've sat through too many nonsensical professional development sessions. I know you have; I've sat through them, too. You have every right to be skeptical about this and to think this is just another one of those things— another waste of your time. I believe in TM and would never waste your time because I know how stressed you sometimes are and how valuable your time is.

I am very aware that you may think TM isn't going to work, that it's some type of religion or cult, that it doesn't make sense, or that it's just stupid. I am asking you to take a leap of faith because this practice has worked for me. If you've never tried it, know that I've been in your shoes. All I knew about TM is what I read on the organization's website and that some very successful people practiced the technique. I took a leap of faith and couldn't be happier in my life.

The National Institutes of Health (NIH) have awarded millions of dollars to research the effectiveness of meditation on stress and stress-related conditions. Hundreds of studies have been conducted at more than 200 independent universities and research institutions, such as Stanford, Harvard, and Yale. In addition, numerous studies have been published in peer-reviewed medical and scientific journals. I was able to find dozens of studies on brain function, cardiovascular health, insomnia, depression, and PTSD. The results of these studies have shown that meditation reduces stress and improves cardiovascular health.

Feeling Optimistic

I always wondered whether I was a pessimistic person by nature. I would question every new initiative, new technique, or new theory that was presented. I now see that I wasn't being negative; I was just being cautious and thoughtful. For example, I would ask questions like these:

- How can I make this work?
- Does this even make sense?
- Why do we have to do it that way?
- Why can't we do it another way?
- Do we really need to do all this paperwork?
- Can this somehow be streamlined?
- Why are we doing this again?
- We already tried it, and it didn't work back then.
- What do we do if this or that happens?

These are just a few examples of the questions that would go through my mind, or that I sometimes asked aloud. I wasn't being negative; I was just trying to make sense of the new initiative and to make sure that it was what's best for students. Listen up administration: Teachers that question are teachers that care. They are not necessarily negative toward the initiative. You just haven't made it make sense for them. Be cautious when labeling someone negative in your mind and try to figure out how to help that person understand the value. The same goes for teachers with their students.

Through my experiences and TM, I learned to see the positive. I try to find the positive in new initiatives before I start questioning them. I'm optimistic about the future. I will continue to question, but I don't allow my mind to go straight to the negative anymore. I see potential. I see opportunity. I see positivity.

How TM Can Help

Transcendental Meditation is NOT about trying to clear your mind. I can't emphasize that enough. It is about much more than that. Though your experiences with TM will be different from mine, I believe that TM can help you supercharge your natural abilities, maximizing your talents and potential. When you begin to meditate, you will find that you become more creative. Your mind will be freed up to design lessons that are more powerful. You will be better positioned to come up with new and better ideas or to solve problems. You also will more easily reflect on your lessons to determine what worked and what didn't.

Many forms of meditation have value. TM is just the technique I chose. It truly is one of the easiest things I have ever learned. I understand that taking my word for it, someone who questions everything and is always skeptical, may be difficult. I'm always looking three steps down the road, trying to rationalize and to be logical about every decision I make. I can't convince you to try TM. You have to want to try it because what you have been doing isn't making you truly feel better. TM is something you have to experience to understand. If TM is not for you, I strongly encourage you to find a form of meditation and physical movement that suits your needs. If you are interested in learning more, the following websites will provide additional information.

- www.tm.org
- www.davidlynchfoundation.org
- www.drtonynader.com
- Cleveland Clinic website
  - my.clevelandclinic.org/health/articles/17906-meditation
  - my.clevelandclinic.org/health/treatments/22292-transcendental-meditation

- **A note from Cleveland Clinic**

  "Transcendental meditation is a type of meditation. You silently repeat a word or phrase in your mind to settle yourself into deep consciousness. Transcendental meditation has been found to have many health benefits, including lowering your blood pressure and reducing stress. If you're interested in exploring transcendental meditation, talk with your healthcare provider about your options."

Appendix B
Statistics and Data

I hate looking at statistics and data so much that I procrastinated putting any in the book. I know they are important, but I would rather someone else analyze the numbers and just tell me what they mean. Yes, of course, we should be data-driven. We need to use data to find out whether what we are doing is working.

However, I would argue that due to the nature of our clientele, we also need to use our experiences, observations, common sense, intuition, and gut instincts. We aren't working with tangible goods. We are working with people, and all humans have the built-in sixth sense—pure consciousness—that secretly helps us. It's the sense that protects us from danger and helps us understand body language, facial expressions, and gestures. We should be using this data as well to help us do a better job teaching our children.

Some folks love data and charts and statistics. That's fantastic, but it isn't me. These topics remind me of two classes I took in grad school. This first was Qualitative and Quantitative

Data and the second was Statistics. For me, these courses were absolutely awful—not because of the professor, but because I have absolutely no interest in these subjects. I was the student who needed remedial instruction. I certainly could have used extended time. Being able to use my notes on the tests sure would have helped. And don't get me started on retakes. Yes, please!!

I digress. The point is that we have all been "that student" at some point in our life. Many of us are just fortunate that wasn't our experience every day of our school career. Data and statistics are my kryptonite. Whenever I think about them, I shudder and don't want anything to do with them. Quite frankly, sometimes I refuse to deal with them. Does that sound like any of your students?

We all have different likes and dislikes, skills, and talents. We should let the people who are good with that kind of stuff thrive, but don't force it on everyone. Did I benefit from the classes I took? Of course, I did. I need to have a basic understanding of stats and data to function in the world; but my livelihood should not be based on whether I passed my stats final exam. The point is that we need to help our children become more well-rounded people, capable of understanding the world they will be asked to make better.

The following notes are included for readers who enjoy data and statistics.

Chapter 1 - Feel Valued

Dewitt, P. (2016, January 26). "Only 46% of students feel valued in their school." *Education Week*. edweek.org.

Quaglia, R. J. (2016). *School voice report 2016*. Quaglia School Voice & Corwin Press. quagliainstitute.org

In a 2016 student voice survey of more than 66,000 students in Grades 6 through 12, some pretty eye-opening information was provided.

- *47% of students felt that they had a voice in their school.*
- *52% of students said that teachers are willing to learn from them.*
- *50% of students said they knew the goals that their school was working on this year.*

About self-worth:

- *46% of students felt that they were a valued member of their school community.*
- *51% thought their teacher would care if they were absent.*
- *60% answered that they were proud of their school.*

About engagement:

- *43% of students said school was boring.*
- *44% of students said their classes help them understand what is happening in their everyday life.*
- *66% said they feel comfortable asking questions in their classes.*

Chapter 2 - Reduce Stress

American Psychological Association. (2018, October). *Stress in America: Generation Z.* Stress in America Survey. apa.org

"The American Psychological Association (APA) conducted its 12th annual Stress in America™ survey in August 2018 to understand what causes stress in Americans' lives and their strategies for coping with stress. The Harris Poll conducted the survey online on behalf of APA among 3,458 respondents ages 18+ living in the United States. In addition to the main sample, interviews among teens ages 15 to 17 (n=300) were collected. This report provides insight into Gen Z, those between the ages of 15 and 21.

Our 2018 survey results show that high-profile issues, such as sexual harassment and gun violence, are significant stressors for Gen Z. America's youngest adults are most likely of all generations to report poor mental health, and Gen Z is also significantly more likely to seek professional help for mental health issues" (APA, 2018, p. 1).

- *91% of Gen Zs between ages 18 and 21 say they have experienced at least one physical or emotional symptom due to stress in the past month compared to 74% of adults overall.*
- *Social Media and Gen Zs:*
  - *55% report feeling supported while on social media.*
  - *45% feel judged on social media.*
  - *38% report feeling bad about themselves on social media.*
- *Three in four Gen Zs report mass shootings as a significant source of stress.*
- *56% of Gen Zs who are in school say they experience stress at least sometimes when considering the possibility of a shooting at their school.*
- *68% of Gen Z adults feel very or somewhat significantly stressed about our nation's future.*
- *50% reported that at least one person they know has been told they are addicted to or have a problem with drugs and alcohol.*
- *25% of Gen Zs say they would not know where to find help if they had a problem with drugs or alcohol.*

- *50% feel they do enough to manage their stress. Additionally, 73% in Gen Z say they could have used more emotional support in the past year.*

- *Additional personal sources of stress for Gen Z (% reporting significant source of stress):*
  - *Bullying/not getting along with others (35%)*
  - *Personal debt (33%)*
  - *Housing instability (31%)*
  - *Hunger/getting enough to eat (28%)*
  - *Drug and alcohol use or addiction in their family (21%)*
  - *Dealing with gender issues relating to their sexual orientation/gender identity (21%)*

Chapter 7 - Avoid the Testing Quicksand

Walker, T. (2016, February 18). Survey: 70 percent of educators say state assessments not developmentally appropriate. *NEA Today. Nea.org*

"Results from a 2015 survey of more than 1500 NEA members teaching the grades and subjects required to be tested under No Child Left Behind (grades 3-8 and 10-12 in ELA and math) indicate that a vast majority of these educators - 70 percent - do not believe their primary state assessment is developmentally appropriate for their students." (Walker, 2016, para. 1)

Teachers Perceptions of Actual vs. "Most Useful" Standardized Tests

	Current Test (PARCC, SBAC, Other)	"Most Useful" Standardized Test
Assesses content that my students have had the opportunity to learn	38.2%	80.8%
Will help me know more about how well my students understand what they have learned	21.8%	73.3%
Will provide feedback to my students that helps them learn	10.7%	72.4%
Will help me set learning goals for individual students	21.2%	69.5%
Accurately assesses my students' progress toward the Common Core or other state standards	25.2%	65.2%
Asks questions in a manner that is developmentally appropriate for my students	13.1%	75.4%
Will provide accurate scores for students with special learning needs	6.2%	70.4%

(Walker, 2016)

Chapter 8 - Challenge Your Gifted Students

Barshay, J. (2021, October 18). *PROOF POINTS: What research tells us about gifted education.* The Hechinger Report. hechingerreport.org

- Percentage of students identified as gifted by ethnicity:
  - Asian – 13%
  - Caucasian – 8%
  - Hispanic – 5%
  - Black – 4%

- A 2012 study found that gifted instruction had no effect on achievement.
  - See https://doi.org/10.1177/0016986211431487

- A 2021 study published in the journal *Educational Evaluation and Policy Analysis* found that gifted programs across the nation provided little to no academic boost.
  - See https://doi.org/10.3102/01623737211008919

Chapter 9 - Pave the Way for Students with Special Needs

The University of Texas Permian Basin. (2022). *Is progress being made toward closing the achievement gap in special education?* https://online.utpb.edu/about-us/articles/education/is-progress-being-made-toward-closing-the-achievement-gap-in-special-education

- "In an article published in the academic journal *Exceptional Children* in 2018, researchers noted a significant achievement gap in American students in grades K-12. This meta-analysis of 23 studies found that on average, students with disabilities performed more than three years below their nondisabled peers. This achievement gap suggests that students with disabilities still have limited access to the instruction needed to succeed in school." (The University of Texas Permian Basin, 2022, para. 3)
  - See full article at https://doi.org/10.1177/0014402918795830

- "One research study published by the American Psychological Association in 2016 looked at the reading comprehension growth trajectories of nearly 100,000 students in grades three through seven. The study found that 'achievement gaps for [students with disabilities] changed very little across grades, and group rankings for the exceptionality groups also remained stable. After four years, none of the groups [of students with disabilities] had "caught up" with the students in [general education] in their reading comprehension achievement.' Expecting all students to reach the same reading level ignores how serious and complex achievement gaps are by the third grade." (The University of Texas Permian Basin, 2022, para. 5)

o   See full article at http://dx.doi.org/10.1037/edu0000107

Chapter 10 - Develop Relationships with Difficult Students

Kessler, R. C., Berglund, P., Demler, O., Jin, R., Merikangas, K. R., & Walters, E. E. (2005). Life-time prevalence and age-of-onset distributions of DSM-IV disorders in the national comorbidity survey replication. *Archives of General Psychiatry 62*(6), 593–602. https://doi.org/10.1001/archpsyc.62.6.593

- Approximately 20% of adolescents have a diagnosable mental health disorder.

Chandra, A., & Minkovitz, C. S. (2006). Stigma starts early: Gender differences in teen willingness to use mental health services. *Journal of Adolescent Health 38*(6), 754e.1–754e8.

https://doi.org/10.1016/j.jadohealth.2005.08.011

- Among adolescents with mental health needs, 70% do not receive the care they need.

Kapphahn, C. J., Morreale, M. C., Rickert, V. I., & Walker, L. R. (2006). Financing mental health services for adolescents: A position paper of the Society for Adolescent Medicine. *Journal of Adolescent Health 39*(3), 456–458.

https://doi.org/10.1016/j.jadohealth.2005.12.013

- Untreated mental health issues may lead to poor school performance, school dropout, strained relationships, involvement with the child welfare or juvenile justice systems, substance abuse, and engagement in risky sexual behaviors.

Data Resource Center for Child & Adolescent Health. (2005/2006). *National survey of children with special health care needs.* The Child and Adolescent Health Measurement Initiative (CAHMI).

https://www.childhealthdata.org/browse/survey

- More than 2 million young people in the United States have emotional/behavioral disabilities (EBD).

- Youth with EBD:
  o have the worst graduation rate of all students with disabilities. Nationally, only 40% of students with EBD graduate from high school, compared to the national average of 76%.
  o are three times as likely as other students to be arrested before leaving school.
  o are twice as likely as other students with other disabilities (e.g., developmental or learning) to be living in a correctional facility, halfway house, drug treatment center, or on the street after leaving school.
  o are twice as likely as students with other disabilities to become teenage mothers.

Chapter 11 - Teach Students to Be Proud Citizens

McClure, M. (2017, March). Tackling the American civics education crisis. *National Conference of State Legislators*, *25*(9).
- According to the 2010 National Assessment of Educational Progress (NAEP) civics report, less than 30%

of fourth-, eighth-, and 12th-grade students are proficient in civics.

- In a 2016 Pew Research Center report, U.S. voter participation came in 31st among 35 developed countries.

- More than 5 million naturalization tests were administered nationwide between 2009 and 2016. For applicants taking both the English and civics tests, the overall national pass rate was 91%.

- "Three major changes helped drive the crisis, according to Dr. Lucian Spataro of the Civics Education Initiative (CEI). First, the country's education system began to focus on science, technology, engineering and math (STEM). 'Parallel to that, standardized testing became the way to measure success and performance. Then, simultaneously, school and teacher funding began to be tied to the results of these tests,' he said. 'These consequences had never before been associated with assessment.' Teaching what is tested became the norm and civics (along with the other 'soft sciences') was deemphasized in the curriculum." (McClure, 2017, para. 3)

For more information:

Hansen, M., Levesque, E., Valant, J., & Quintero, D. (2018, June). *The 2018 Brown Center report on American education: How well are American students learning?* Brown Center of Education Policy at Brookings. Brookings Institute.

https://www.brookings.edu/wp-content/uploads/2018/06/2018-Brown-Center-Report-on-American-Education_FINAL1.pdf

Chapter 12 - Instill a Love of Learning

National Soft Skills Association. (2020, March 9). *Study: Boosting soft skills is better than raising test scores.*

https://www.nationalsoftskills.org/boosting-test-scores

- "A recent study was just released by Northwestern University's Kirabo Jackson on the effect of soft skills vs test scores. This study demonstrates that schools that build social-emotional qualities are getting better short-term and long-term results for students than schools that only focus on improving test scores. This study included 150,000 high school students in all 133 Chicago Public

Schools from 2008 onward, and reported that schools putting soft skills ahead of test scores produced students with higher grades, fewer absences and fewer disciplinary problems and arrests in high school. The students who attended these high schools also graduated and went to college at higher rates." (National Soft Skills Association, 2020, para. 1)

See full report at https://hechingerreport.org/early-research-focuses-on-schools-that-develop-students-social-emotional-qualities

National Soft Skills Association. (2019, July 8). *Why soft skills are so difficult to teach.* https://www.nationalsoftskills.org/why-soft-skills-are-so-difficult-to-teach

- "A lot has happened in the field of soft skills over the last few years. Awareness of the need for employees to possess soft skills such as attitude, communication, critical thinking, and professionalism, to name a few, has begun to reach a fevered pitch. High school career and technology education (CTE) programs as well as post-secondary institutions have identified the need to offer training in soft skills.

- There are hidden skills or competencies that are needed as the foundation blocks upon which soft skills can be taught. These necessary building blocks are known as emotional intelligence or EQ. EQ is a learned ability to identify, explain, understand and express human emotions in healthy and productive ways. Without these foundation blocks, a learner's ability to understand and to use soft skills is very limited.

- The core EQ foundation skills needed in order to develop these interpersonal skills are self-esteem, interpersonal awareness, empathy and a supportive environment." (National Soft Skills Association, 2019, paras. 1, 2, 5)

Price, A. (2010). *What are the benefits for teaching and learning of cross-curricular work using thinking skills, techniques, and languages?* National Teacher Research Panel.
http://www.curee.co.uk/files/RMHolyRosary/Resources/What_are_the_benefits_for_teaching_and_learning_of_cross_curricular_work.pdf

Summary of main findings:

- The quality of numerous areas of pupil learning improved, including questioning, self and group reflection, sharing of ideas, consensus, and awareness of task requirements.

- Some students (from across the attainment range) became increasingly aware of the "thinking skills" they were using. A minority became confident at transferring their use into different contexts.

- A general rise in confidence occurred among the students in tackling tasks, making suggestions, and criticizing assumptions.
- Gabriel, J. (n.d.) *The benefits of cross-curricular instruction.* https://sites.google.com/site/professionalpageofjohngabriel/home/the-benefits-of-cross-curricular-instruction

- "Traditionally, students have studied subjects in isolation, but this leads to fragmentary knowledge and a disconnection of applying the material practically. Students need to see the relationships within and between disciplines. Each subject is a slice of the whole. Connecting the slices leads to synergistic learning.

- Cross-curricular instruction offers the following advantages to students: increased motivation, improvement of the learning process, genuine teamwork, and pathways for further discoveries. When teachers take the additional step of branching out into other disciplines and relating theory to the real-world, they are able to entice their students to embrace the subject matter. Once students learn how to apply their knowledge, they begin to see the value in learning. A greater appreciation of the learning process leads students to become active-stakeholders and life-long learners.

- Through interdisciplinary studies, students are able to collaborate with one another. We, humans, are social beings; therefore, positive interaction serves as enhancement for acquiring new knowledge. Teamwork paves the way for new discoveries. It allows the students to share realizations and new ideas. Group members can experience multiple viewpoints, which lead to a better understanding of the material and human interaction." (Gabriel, n.d., paras. 1, 3, 5)

Appendix C

Further Reading

I suppose I generalized a bit when talking about experts, academics, and authors of books on education. Don't get me wrong; there are numerous outstanding authors and researchers. I just wanted to point out that writing a book or publishing an article doesn't automatically make anybody an expert. We need to be more judicious when adopting new theories or strategies. Following are a few books for your consideration that I found to be insightful and thought-provoking.

- Daniel H. Pink: *Drive: The Surprising Truth About What Motivates Us*
- James W. Loewen: *Lies My Teacher Told Me: Everything Your American History Textbook Got Wrong*
- Todd G. Gongwer: *Lead . . . for God's Sake: A Parable for Finding the Heart of Leadership*
- Greg McKeown: *Essentialism: The Disciplined Pursuit of Less*

Appendix D

Examples of 4-Day Calendars

In Chapter 11, I proposed changing the school calendar. Following are two examples of possible school schedules. I'm really not sure which option I prefer. With Option A, students and staff never have to work more than 2 days in a row before a short break. Unfortunately, this option provides fewer extended breaks, but it does have smaller, more periodic breaks.

- 172 Student Days
- 11 Teacher Work Days
- First and Last Student Days = 2
- Open House or Parent Teacher Conference Nights
  (0.5 days each)
- Total Teacher Work Days = 185

Option B might have a slight edge over Option A for me personally. Every weekend is a 4-day weekend. Need I say more? I think the main reason this takes the slight lead is because it offers a little more extended vacation time throughout the year. This could incentivize families to schedule vacations around the extended breaks so they can miss as little or even no school days.

- 175 Student Days
- 8 Teacher Work Days
- First and Last Student Days = 2
- Open House or Parent Teacher Conference Nights (0.5 days each)
- Total Teacher Work Days = 185

Option A

JUNE 2021

M	T	W	TH	F
	1	2	3	4
7	8	9	10	11
14	15	16	17	18
21	22	23	24	25
28	29	30		

JULY 2021

M	T	W	TH	F
			1	2
5	6	7	8	9
12	13	14	15	16
19	20	21	22	23
26	27	28	29	30

AUGUST 2021

M	T	W	TH	F
2	3	4	5	6
9	10	11	12	13
16	17	18	19	20
23	24	25	26	27
30	31			

SEPTEMBER 2021

M	T	W	TH	F
		1	2	3
6	7	8	9	10
13	14	15	16	17
20	21	22	23	24
27	28	29	30	

OCTOBER 2021

M	T	W	TH	F
				1
4	5	6	7	8
11	12	13	14	15
18	19	20	21	22
25	26	27	28	29

NOVEMBER 2021

M	T	W	TH	F
1	2	3	4	5
8	9	10	11	12
15	16	17	18	19
22	23	24	25	26
29	30			

DECEMBER 2021

M	T	W	TH	F
		1	2	3
6	7	8	9	10
13	14	15	16	17
20	21	22	23	24
27	28	29	30	31

JANUARY 2022

M	T	W	TH	F
3	4	5	6	7
10	11	12	13	14
17	18	19	20	21
24	25	26	27	28
31				

FEBRUARY 2022

M	T	W	TH	F
	1	2	3	4
7	8	9	10	11
14	15	16	17	18
21	22	23	24	25
28				

MARCH 2022

M	T	W	TH	F
	1	2	3	4
7	8	9	10	11
14	15	16	17	18
21	22	23	24	25
28	29	30	31	

APRIL 2022

M	T	W	TH	F
				1
4	5	6	7	8
11	12	13	14	15
18	19	20	21	22
25	26	27	28	29

MAY 2022

M	T	W	TH	F
2	3	4	5	6
9	10	11	12	13
16	17	18	19	20
23	24	25	26	27
30	31			

172 Student Days
△ 11 Teacher Work Days

4 Open House or Parent Teacher Conference Nights (0.5 days each)
First and Last Student Days

Total Teacher Work Days = 185

197

Option B

JUNE 2021

M	T	W	TH	F
	1	2	3	4
7	8	9	10	11
14	15	16	17	18
21	22	23	24	25
28	29	30		

JULY 2021

M	T	W	TH	F
			1	2
5	6	7	8	9
12	13	14	15	16
19	20	21	22	23
26	27	28	29	30

AUGUST 2021

M	T	W	TH	F
2	3	4	5	6
9	10	11	12	13
16	17	18	19	20
23	24	25	26	27
30	31			

SEPTEMBER 2021

M	T	W	TH	F
		1	2	3
6	7	8	9	10
13	14	15	16	17
20	21	22	23	24
27	28	29	30	

OCTOBER 2021

M	T	W	TH	F
				1
4	5	6	7	8
11	12	13	14	15
18	19	20	21	22
25	26	27	28	29

NOVEMBER 2021

M	T	W	TH	F
1	2	3	4	5
8	9	10	11	12
15	16	17	18	19
22	23	24	25	26
29	30			

DECEMBER 2021

M	T	W	TH	F
		1	2	3
6	7	8	9	10
13	14	15	16	17
20	21	22	23	24
27	28	29	30	31

JANUARY 2022

M	T	W	TH	F
3	4	5	6	7
10	11	12	13	14
17	18	19	20	21
24	25	26	27	28
31				

FEBRUARY 2022

M	T	W	TH	F
	1	2	3	4
7	8	9	10	11
14	15	16	17	18
21	22	23	24	25
28				

MARCH 2022

M	T	W	TH	F
	1	2	3	4
7	8	9	10	11
14	15	16	17	18
21	22	23	24	25
28	29	30	31	

APRIL 2022

M	T	W	TH	F
				1
4	5	6	7	8
11	12	13	14	15
18	19	20	21	22
25	26	27	28	29

MAY 2022

M	T	W	TH	F
2	3	4	5	6
9	10	11	12	13
16	17	18	19	20
23	24	25	26	27
30	31			

175 Student Days
△ 8 Teacher Work Days

4 Open House or Parent Teacher Conference Nights (0.5 days each)
O First and Last Student Days

Total Teacher Work Days = 185